iPhone

Fully Loaded

iPhone
Fully Loaded

Andy Ihnatko

WILEY

Wiley Publishing, Inc.

iPhone® Fully Loaded

Published by
Wiley Publishing, Inc.
111 River Street
Hoboken, N.J. 07030
www.wiley.com

Published by Wiley Publishing, Inc., Indianapolis, Indiana
Published simultaneously in Canada

Library of Congress Control Number: 2007938872

ISBN: 978-0-470-17368-8

Manufactured in the United States of America

10 9 8 7 6 5 4 3 2 1

For general information on our other products and services or to obtain technical support, please contact our Customer Care Department within the U.S. at (800) 762-2974, outside the U.S. at (317) 572-3993 or fax (317) 572-4002.

Wiley also publishes its books in a variety of electronic formats. Some content that appears in print may not be available in electronic books.

Colophon: This book was produced using the Adobe Garamond typeface for the body copy and the Myriad Pro typeface for the headlines.

Acknowledgments

Most of you haven't written a book, but the majority of you have had mothers at one time or another. I'm here to tell you that the awesome power of giving your mom the Number 1 spot in the Acknowledgments page of a book you've written cannot possibly be underestimated.

The effect is immediate and dramatic and I fully intend to keep the gravy train of free homemade spaghetti sauce and biscotti coming with every new book I write.

But shout-outs are also very much due to the editors on this project: Courtney Allen, Galen Gruman, and Carol Person. Life is hard for an author who wants to write damned-useful guide to getting the most out of a brand-new product, but rain falls into the lives of the editors of such a book as well. Many's the time when I had to tell them, "You know that chapter I sent you six weeks ago? I'm scrapping it and doing it over again" because the world had changed so much. During the final couple of weeks of production, I was pulling back previously edited chapters nearly as fast as I was writing them.

Some people think that the easy availability of weapons in this country is a good thing and some think it's a bad thing. All I can say is that it makes it very easy for editors to indulge their dark interior fantasies of mayhem and vengeance. The fact that I am here and healthy is a testament to my editors' commitment to not interfering in the completion or excellence of this book. Although now that my work is done, I'm just going to make myself scarce for a few weeks.

Props to my agent, Carole McClendon, and to Simon Pope of Apple. And to all of the iPhone's and iPod Touch's designers and developers.

Finally, my thanks to the one awesome higher power responsible for everything good in this world, without whom I would be nothing but a puddle of useless enzymes: Coca-Cola.

Credits

Acquisitions Editor
Courtney Allen

Editorial Manager
Robyn B. Siesky

**Vice President &
Executive Group Publisher**
Richard Swadley

Vice President and Publisher
Barry Pruett

Business Manager
Amy Knies

Marketing Manager
Sandy Smith

Project and Layout Editor
Galen Gruman, The Zango Group

Editor
Carol Person, The Zango Group

Production Designer
Jonathan Woolson, thinkplaydesign

Book Designer
Galen Gruman, The Zango Group

Cover Image
Michael Trent

**Copy Editing, Proofreading, and
Indexing**
The Zango Group

About the Author

The Wikipedia entry for Andy Ihnatko categorizes him as "Living Person — American Journalist." That's just about right.

He's been writing regular columns about technology since 1989, contributing to mainstream publications as well as every magazine that ever carried the prefix "Mac-." He's currently a regular columnist for *Macworld*, MacObserver.com, and a regular panelist on the popular *MacBreak-Weekly* and *This Week in Technology* (TWiT) podcasts. When he can afford to get his good jacket out of the cleaners, he makes appearances on the *CBS Early Show*, too.

His weekly tech column in *The Chicago Sun-Times* is worthy of a Pulitzer. But just try convincing the Pulitzer committee. Seriously. Andy's tried and failed. And he wants that Pulitzer *so damned badly.* If you wear that Pulitzer medallion around your neck, you can park wherever the hell you want. If you're ever in Chicago and you see a Mercedes parked across two handicapped spaces and part of the sidewalk, you know Roger Ebert must be nearby.

Andy is good to his parents, is kind to animals, donates blood regularly, and returns his library books on time. He lives in Boston with his two goldfish, Click and Drag.

You can visit Andy's Web site (featuring his blog and e-mail links) at www.ihnatko.com.

Contents

INTRODUCTION   XVII

PART 1: THE BASICS OF CONTENT   1

Chapter 1: Remedial iTunes   3

Chapter 2: How To Make 8 Gigabytes Seem Like 80   13

PART III: THE INTERNET   75

Chapter 9: News, Blogs, and Bookmarks   77

Chapter 10: What a Friend We Have in RSS   91

Chapter 11: Software, Kind Of (and No, Really)   101

Chapter 12: Sticking Web Pages in Your Ear   117

Chapter 13: Podcasts   123

Chapter 14: Audio Streams   139

Chapter 15: Internet Videos   155

Contents

Introduction

I really *do* enjoy these little conversations between you (dear, dear reader) and me. You know? You haven't really started reading the book yet, we haven't finished our drinks, we're all just sort of milling about here in the lobby and enjoying a pleasant conversation before we head on into the conference room where I give you your mandatory safety training and explain the office evacuation plan.

Figuratively speaking, of course. In truth — oh, do you need that topped off? No? Good, good, well, the rest of the bottle is right over there if you change your mind — I know that you fall into one of two categories:

A happy purchaser of this book. In which case I need to thank you *very* kindly because your royalty contribution will go towards keeping my Mom convinced that I have an actual job. This is an uphill struggle at the best of days. You would understand this if you saw my car.

I also reassure you that one day you shall look back fondly on this purchase and flag it in your memory as one of the smartest decisions you ever made.

Someone who doesn't actually own this book, but who is apparently leafing through it anyway. I'm talking about you people loafing around in the bookstore, mostly. That's a fairly strong demographic and I'm very wise to welcome you people specifically. Back when I was a kid, you didn't get that sort of traffic through a book's introduction. Bookstores were independently owned businesses operated by lonely and bitter people who took one look at me in my cutoff jeans and growled, "Why don't you just roll right back on outta here like the tide?"

Now (thank heavens), enormous, careless megacorporations have driven independent booksellers out of business. They're usually staffed by poorly paid hourly employees who honestly don't give a damn if you stay there all day and make it all the way through the first seven volumes of *The Complete Peanuts* by Charles Schulz. Hell, they even give you comfy chairs, an in-store coffee bar, and a public bathroom. If these bookstores made a point of hiring former interdenominational military chaplains as management, people wouldn't even have to leave for high holidays and holy days of obligation.

Oh! I *suppose* you could be at a friend's house, sneaking a look through his or her library. If this is a first-date situation, I'd definitely consider letting them get to first base with you at minimum.

First, owning this book definitively identifies him or her as a being of unparalleled taste, intelligence, kindness, maturity, and insight. Also, they clearly like to read up on how to do things the *right* way. If you know what I mean.

Second, if word gets out that "if you buy Ihnatko's book, he'll help you get some serious smoochin'," this can only help sales.

If it's not a first-date situation and you're just looking to steal a few things, please *do* go ahead and take this book. It's chockablock with useful info and, if it goes missing, I'm sure they'll buy another copy, which will *also* push my numbers up.

THE POINT OF ALL THIS

However I happen to have gained your attention, thanks for reading.

Like the other books in my "Fully Loaded" series, the purpose of this book is not to give you a ground-up explanation of how the iPhone or the iPod Touch works. The philosophy of this series has always been that there are already way too many books out there that teach you the usual stuff. Like how (using the iPhone as an example) to download your e-mail and how to add new bookmarks to the Web browser and that if you hold your finger on the virtual keyboard's

Symbols key and drag it across the keyboard instead of tapping, the Symbol keyboard will appear and if you lift your finger when it's on top of the key you want, you'll have your QWERTY keyboard back without tapping any more buttons.

Oh, that wasn't in the iPhone book you already had?

Awesome. Well, that's a bonus.

No, the goal of "Fully Loaded" has always been to look upon a device like the iPhone as an empty vessel that you can fill to the brim with every type of material you need or want in your personal or professional life. The iPhone is a pretty damned scary-crazy-nice bit of tech, but just because the manual says nothing about synching YouTube videos on it, or storing Microsoft Office documents, or converting your e-mails into podcasts that you can listen to during your morning commute doesn't mean that you can't do any of those things with it.

It just means that you need the *knack*. And my honorable and trustworthy friend — you burglars there in the audience, I don't mean you so much, obviously — you can call me Doug Fieger.

Doug Fieger. You know? Founder and lead singer for The Knack? "My Sharona" was probably their biggest hit.

Okay, that's not really important. The point is that if you're looking for the basic stuff that you can either get from any other book or from just fooling around with your iPhone for a week, this isn't the book for you.

This book is for people who want someone to ask them, "Wait, how did you get *Raiders of the Lost Ark* on your iPhone? That movie isn't in the iTunes store!" The questioner will approach with trembling hands that daren't touch the hem of your robe for fear of being reduced to ash by the awesome power bottled within your corporeal form.

Oh, and if you own an iPod Touch instead of an iPhone, jump right in — the water's just fine. Not *everything* in this book will apply to you but you'll find that any technique or trick that relies on the music, video, or photo viewers on your iPod, or that relies on the Safari browser, will work just fine on an iPod Touch. That's a pretty big chunk of the book.

Hang on, I'll actually look through the outline. Yes, every chapter has content that benefits iPod Touch users as well as iPhone users. You're out of luck on those few bits that require the use of the Mail app, and there a few more gaps here and there, but on the whole I'd say this book is just up your street. It's just that the book goes a few more blocks for iPhone users.

I think I've said everything I wanted to say here. Let's get started.

But first, some final words for …

The Bookstore Browser. Let's see. I think if you flip to Chapter 4 (ripping DVDs), and then maybe Chapter 19 (putting any information you want onto your iPhone, despite the fact that iTunes limits you to just music, video, and photos), and finally Chapter 10 (RSS, one of my most favorite chapters), you'll feel as though the purchase price of this book is a shrewd and safe investment.

The Guest in Someone's House, Possibly in a First-Date Situation. Again, cover that man or women with mad monkey smooches as though a forty-cent tax on kisses goes into effect in ten minutes. He or she deserves it. Also, you'd be doing me a big solid if you discreetly ripped out all of the chapters I mentioned in the preceding paragraph. They're some of the best bits of the book, so

the person's bound to buy a new copy. Plus you'll read them at home and like the book so much buy a copy of your own to get those missing chapters. Two more royalties for Andy. Awesome.

Plus, when they come to *your* house, they'll spot the book on your shelf and say, "No way! You have that book, too?" You can play it either as "Wow, we must *totally* have the same taste in everything!" or "Yup! I looked at it on your shelf and was so impressed that I bought my own copy. You sure know how to find useful, unique things!"

This person might have an all-expenses-paid company retreat to Kauai coming up, and maybe they're allowed to bring a guest. If so, this sort of sense of kismet will urge them to bring you instead of their mom.

The Burglar. Remember, police response time is typically about two and a half minutes. So take the book and *go*, already. I've just Googled for information on alarm codes and it seems that the default disarm password for the two most popular home security systems are 2287 and 1111.

Just remember who your friends are. Maybe you could tear out those three chapters and leave the book and the chapters in the next two houses you rob? Again, I'm convinced that your next victims will be so taken by the incomplete book that they'll both buy fresh copies.

Which means more royalties for me, which means I can finally afford one of those big HDTVs, which means that you'll *finally* find something worth stealing if you break into my house.

Which you shouldn't do, because remember, I helped you with those security codes and everything. All right?

OH YEAH, THAT BORING, PRACTICAL STUFF

Well, I can't say I'm a fan of conventions because they are so … er … conventional. But even I, despite all my sheer force of personality, must sometimes bow to conventions. Like for all those geeky aspects inevitable in a book that talks about computer technology, so you know what I mean when I diverge from good ol' English. Wherever possible, I've kept the book free of weird computer symbols and geeky icons. But some insisted on being used, so here are their conventions.

Mouse Conventions

Here's what I mean when I talk about using the mouse:

- Click: Most Mac mice have only one button, but some have two or more; all PC mice have at least two buttons. If you have a multibutton mouse, quickly press and release the leftmost mouse button once when I say to click the mouse. (If your mouse has only one button — you guessed it — just press and release the button you have.)
- Double-click: When I say to double-click, quickly press and release the leftmost mouse button twice (if your mouse has only one button, just press and release twice the button you have). On some multibutton mice, one of the buttons can function as a double-click (you click it once, the mouse clicks twice); if your mouse has this feature, use it — it saves strain on your hand.
- Right-click: A Windows feature since Windows 95, right-clicking means clicking the right-hand mouse button. On a Mac's one-button mouse, hold the Control key when clicking the mouse button to achieve the right-click effect. On multibutton Mac mice, Mac OS X automatically assigns the righthand button to Control+click.
- Tap: This is the equivalent of clicking on a touchscreen, using your finger or stylus rather than a mouse.
- Drag: Dragging is used for moving and sizing items in a document. To drag an item, position the mouse pointer on it. Press and hold down the mouse button, and then slide the mouse across a flat surface to drag the item. Release the mouse button to drop the dragged item in its new location.

The commands that you select by using the program menus appear in this book in normal typeface. When you choose some menu commands, a related pull-down menu or a pop-up menu appears. If I describe a situation in which you need to select one menu and then choose a command from a secondary menu or list box, I use an arrow symbol. For example, "Choose Edit ▸ Paste" means that you should choose the Paste command from the Edit menu.

Keyboard Conventions

In those rare cases where I get into nitty-gritty computer commands, I'll provide both the Windows and Macintosh shortcuts throughout, with the Windows shortcut first. In most cases, the Windows and Mac shortcuts are the same, except for the names of the keys, as follows:

- The Windows Ctrl key is the most-used shortcut key. Its Mac equivalent is the Command key, which is indicated on keyboards and program menus (and thus in this book) by the symbol ⌘.

▣ Shift is the same on the Mac and Windows. In many Mac program menus, Shift is displayed by the symbol ⇧.

▣ The Option key on the Mac is usually the same as the Alt key in Windows. In many Mac program menus — including iTunes — you'll see the symbol ⌥ used.

▣ The Control key on the Mac has no Windows equivalent (it is *not* the same as the Windows Ctrl key). Many Mac programs indicate it with the symbol ⌃ in their menus.

▣ The Tab key is used both to move within fields in panels and dialog boxes and to insert the tab character in text. iTunes and many other Mac programs indicate it in menus with the symbol ⇥.

▣ The Enter key (Windows) or Return key (Mac) is used to apply a dialog box's settings and close the dialog box (equivalent to clicking OK or Done), as well as to insert a hard paragraph return in text. In many Mac programs, it is indicated in menus by the symbol ↵. Note that there is another key labeled Enter on most keyboards, in the numeric keypad. This keypad Enter usually works like the regular Return or Enter.

▣ The Delete key (Mac) and Backspace key (Windows) deletes text, one character at a time, to the left of the text-insertion point. On the Mac, programs like iTunes use the symbol ⌫ to indicate Delete. Windows also has a separate Delete key that deletes text, on character at a time, to the right of the text-insertion point. The Mac's Clear key, although in the same position on the keyboard, does not delete text.

If you're supposed to press several keys at the same time, I indicate that by placing plus signs (+) between them. Thus, Shift+⌘+A means press and hold the Shift and ⌘ keys, then press A. After you've pressed the A key, let go of all three keys. (You don't need to hold down the last letter in the sequence.)

I also use the plus sign (+) to join keys to mouse movements. For example, Alt+drag means to hold the Alt key while dragging the mouse in Windows , and Option+drag means to hold the Option key while dragging the mouse on the Mac.

Rarely, I indicate programming code or text you must enter as is into some dialog box or other program interface. I do that by formatting the text in a typewriter-like font: like this.

Okay, enough of this techno-mumbo-jumbo. Onto the good stuff!

PART I

The Basics of Content

Remedial iTunes

The Skim

This is going to sound odd, but I'm going to start the first real chapter of this book by saying mean things about a teacher.

Well, look, the news is still fresh and it sort of stings. I spent the summer helping my niece with her summer reading. She was assigned a pretty interesting and meaty book, and we got together for six half-hour sessions to discuss the characters, the tone, the larger issues, the background, everything. Together, we read the holy *hell* out of that book.

Today was the first day of school. And what do you think happened? The teacher hit everybody with a pop exam about the book. And there weren't any *interesting* questions, either, like "Do you suppose the author approved of the choices made by the lead character?" No, it was full of football trivia, like asking who said a certain line, or what is the French word for *Velcro*?

My beloved niece got rooked and rooked good by a woman who is clearly unhappy with the behavior of her *own* kids but can't bear to inflict suffering on her own flesh and blood. Sad. So very sad.

I bring this up, of course, to make me appear that much more terrific in your eyes. Because here on page one of Chapter 1, it's like it's the first day of school. What's Mr. Ihnatko going to do with his class? Relax. I just want you to relax and tell me how your summer went. Let's spend this first day going over remedial stuff, just to make sure that we all start off on the same page. Literally.

This introduction has now gone on for so long that I'm fairly certain that it's spilled over onto page 2 or 3. I admit this manfully and openly, accepting the consequences unafraid. Golly, that's yet *another* reason for you to be impressed with me! This is great!

So herewith is a little course in remedial iTunes, since that's the engine that gets most of the cool stuff on your iPhone or iPod Touch.

After this chapter, if I glibly end a long technical process by dismissively saying, "And then drag the video file into iTunes or add it to a playlist," please mentally cut and paste this entire chapter into the space allotted by that short phrase.

TIDBIT

Creating playlists isn't absolutely necessary; your iPhone allows you to idly browse your content by artist, album title, etc.

But as advanced as its technology is, your iPhone has no way of knowing that *these* 11 songs, played in *this* specific order constitute the ultimate make out mix tape.

Without your guidance, *Tony Bennett and Bill Evans: Together Again* always begins with Track 1 and ends with Track 18, and doesn't skip over songs like "You Don't Know What Love Is," which I think you'll agree will totally destroy the mood.

THE VERY VERY (VERY) BASICS

The one slight bummer about the iPhone and the iPod Touch is that you, the humble hard-working user, are never allowed to access the device directly. Those tawdry little players made by vulgar other companies are like little hard drives that let you store music and video files. Whether you're using a Windows PC or a Mac, you just drag files into the device's open folder and, bango, the device figures out what to do with the files.

You can use a desktop app to speed up the process, but really, it isn't complicated.

For a million reasons — some in your bests interests, some not — Apple doesn't give you that same courtesy with the iPhone and iPod Touch. The iTunes app always, always, *always* acts as the gatekeeper. The iTunes app acts as a library for all your media (see Figure 1-1). You then selectively tell iTunes what content you'd like to have on your device, and then iTunes does all the sorting and moving for you.

So the path from A File On Your Hard Drive to A Music Or Video File Or Photo That You Can Tap On And Enjoy On Your Device goes like this:

◘ You import the file into iTunes, which adds it to its huge and ever-increasing catalogue of music and video.

◘ You organize your content into playlists.

◘ You tell iTunes which content should be automatically copied to your iPhone's media library.

◘ Your iPhone is updated with fresh content when you plug it into your computer. This can happen automatically as soon as iTunes realizes that the iPhone (or iPod Touch) has been plugged in, or if you're the sort of control freak who

Figure 1-1
iTunes: the center of our iPhone passion play

won't let an employee have a pad of freaking sticky notes without filling out a form, you can explicitly tell iTunes to update the thing *right now*.

IMPORTING FILES INTO ITUNES

iTunes isn't a simple music player — it's not just an app that just plays a file off your hard drive and then forgets that it ever existed. No, iTunes is grabby and ambitious: It's a Media Content Library Management System. When you import a music or video file into iTunes, information about the file is added to a master database so that you can locate one song among thousands in an instant (a seven-minute version of "Anarchy

in the U.K." recorded by Buddy Ebsen) and unless you've explicitly told iTunes not to organize your library for you — ach, those control freak issues, yet again — iTunes will also copy the file into its own special music directory.

There are two different ways to add files to your iTunes library:

Method the First: Use the Add to Library Command

1. Choose File ▶ Add To Library.
   - ◻ In the Windows edition of iTunes, there are two Add to Library menu items. Add File allows you to select one specific file. If you choose Add Folder, iTunes will scan through

the contents of a selected folder and automatically add any music or video files that it's capable of playing.

- ◻ In the Macintosh version of iTunes, a single command that handles both tasks. Either way, you'll find yourself looking at your computer's standard file/folder browser.

2. Select a music or video file, or a folder containing music and videos.

3. Click the highlighted button. On a Mac, it'll be Choose. If you're selecting a file on a PC, it'll be OK, or Open if you're using the Add Folder command.

iTunes will percolate for a minute. When it's finished, all the selected files that it formats that iTunes understands will appear in the iTunes library.

Method the Second: Just Drag It

If you're in Windows Explorer or the Mac Finder and you can see the name or icon of the files you want to import, you just drag the files straight into iTunes without any further ado. Drag them into the iTunes window, drag them into iTunes's desktop icon or its tile in the Windows taskbar or the Macintosh dock. However you do it, if iTunes

Figure 1-2
A new playlist takes its first breath.

thinks it knows how to handle the file, a plus sign (+) will appear next to your mouse pointer when you enter iTunes's airspace. Release, and iTunes will take it from there.

ORGANIZING YOUR MUSIC INTO PLAYLISTS

Using playlists brings two big boons. Yes, it's handy to be able to instantly access a collection of songs tailor-made for workouts, an evening of romance, or piloting your souped-up Dodge Charger down rural backroads at breakneck speeds with Boss Hogg in close pursuit. But it also helps you manage the problem of having more music and video than you have space for on your device. The goal of this book is to help you stuff that device until it's ready to a-splode; if you have so little content that you have no need for playlists, then I'll somehow feel as though I haven't done my job.

You can create as many different playlists as you like. iTunes offers them in two flavors: (a) the plain-vanilla variety, through which you manually select specific music and video, and (b) synchs, through which you simply describe the *sort* of music you'd like to hear, and trust iTunes to work out the specific details.

Plain Old Playlists

You can create a new playlist either by choosing File ▶ New Playlist or by click-

TIP

The scope of the Add To Library command is not limited to just folders. If someone hands you a CD or a DVD filled with MP3 files, for instance, you can use your computer's file/folder browser to select the entire volume.

ing the plus (+) button at the bottom of the iTunes browser window. Either way, an untitled playlist will appear in iTunes's list of music sources (see Figure 1-2).

Untitled Playlist (the default playlist name) is highlighted and awaits your creative genius. Type in something a little more memorable. "Just Drive" is my usual playlist of stuff I want to hear in the car.

And that's really all there is to it. Any songs I drag into Just Drive will be added to the playlist, viz:

1. Click on Library in the iTunes window's Sources list. A list of all the music and video in your iTunes library appears.
2. Select one or more items from your library.
3. Drag them over the playlist's name.

Incidentally, when you copy items into a playlist the only thing you're actually copying is the items' information. All your actual music and video files remain where they were in iTunes's library, which means that a music track or video can be in many different playlists all at once.

Honestly, I mean, what sort of life would it be if we could only enjoy "The Cockroach That Ate Cincinnati" in one playlist at a time?

If you click on the playlist's name, iTunes's browser window will switch to a view of that playlist's tracks. You can change the play order of those items by dragging them around, or remove items by selecting them and then hitting the Backspace or Delete key on your keyboard.

Smart Playlists

There are certain features of certain apps that make me seriously want to stick five

> **TIP**
>
> You can automatically create a new playlist from a group of selected tracks in one step. On a Mac, you simply drag the group into any empty spot in the Sources section of the iTunes window. If you're not dragging 'em into an existing playlist, iTunes assumes that you want to make a new one with these items. In the Windows edition, select a group of items and then choose File ▶ New Playlist from Selection.

bucks in an envelope and mail it to the company. The smart playlist is definitely one of those features.

Smart playlists allow you to create a playlist without being specific about its contents. You describe the *sort* of content you want and iTunes makes the selections for you. iTunes stores a lot of information about all the items in its library — including how frequently and recently you've been playing that stuff — which means that it's easy to get iTunes to make some fairly sophisticated choices on your behalf.

For instance: I buy lots of music through the iTunes Music Store, representing different artists and genres. And every time I take my hour long constitutional — I'd *like* to call it a "morning jog" but that would imply an ability to run faster than the average man can walk on his hands — I want to listen to my latest tunes.

I could either religiously move tracks in and out of a manual playlist or just define a Smart Playlists by choosing File ▶ New Smart Playlist (see Figure 1-3).

Figure 1-3

A smart playlist that selects music for my morning constitutional

can alternatively tell iTunes to limit the number of songs or the amount of space the collection will take up. I've also told it to select the newest songs. I could have asked iTunes to pick songs at random, songs that I haven't heard recently, or choose from an abundance of other options.

After I click OK, the new smart playlist will be automatically populated with items that match all the rules I've laid out (see Figure 1-4).

Each line represents a different "rule" to apply when choosing songs; to add a new one, I click the plus (+) button at the end of any rule. This smart playlist says:

- Kind, Contains, Protected: Chooses only protected songs, meaning copy-protected songs, which means songs purchased through the iTunes Store.
- Genre Does Not Contain, Audiobook: Don't choose any spoken-word recordings or books-on-tape. Neither my metabolism nor my enthusiasm for exercise are great enough to keep my legs moving during 45 minutes of Alan Greenspan's memoirs.
- Time, Is Greater Than, 6:00: For that matter, don't select any music over six minutes long, either.
- Last Played, Is Not in the Last, 3, Days: If I've played this song any time in the last three days, don't bother playing it again. My attention span is desperately short.

Under that list of rules, there's also line to specify how much music you'd like, and how you'd like iTunes to make the selection. One hour will do me just fine, though you

And one of the (many) terrific features of smart playlists is that the playlist is "live." If for whatever reason a track inside a synch no longer meets your list of rules, zap! It's removed from the playlist and replaced with one that does. My "Constitutional" playlist always contains my newest tracks. If I buy three new songs from the iTunes store, they'll be added to the playlist automagically and the oldest songs in the playlist will be kicked out to make room for them.

(Just like the oldest cast members on *Survivor.*)

UPDATING YOUR IPHONE OR IPOD TOUCH

When you connect your device to your computer, it automatically appears in iTunes's list of music sources. What happens after that depends on the iPhone Options or iPod Options you've set. (I'll just call it "iPhone Options" from here on out, okay?)

You can open the iPhone Options window by clicking on your iPhone's name in the Devices section of the iTunes window. You wind up with a window like the one you see in Figure 1-5.

Figure 1-4
Presto! iTunes is your personal deejay, choosing tunes based on your general likes.

iTunes will update the iPhone's contents automatically every time you plug it in, if you leave the Automatically Sync When This Phone is Connected checkbox checked.

There's another tweak to all this: the Sync Only Checked Songs and Videos checkbox. Each video track in every iTunes window has a checkbox next to it. When this option is enabled, any item that *does not* have its checkbox checked will not be synched to your device, which makes it easy to "point and shoot" certain items that you never want to hear in the car.

Automatic updates only take place when you plug in your device. You can also tell iTunes to update this device *right freaking now* by clicking the Sync button. You'd use Sync if you've added new items or playlist to

your iTunes library since plugging in your iPhone.

You'll note that the Options window is organized into tabs. There's one for each different type of media that you can load up on your device.

Use the Music tab to tell iTunes precisely which bits of your music (or video, or photo,

TIDBIT

Be sure to check out Chapter 2. It contains some simple tricks for making the limited capacity of your iPhone or iPod Touch seem irrelevant.

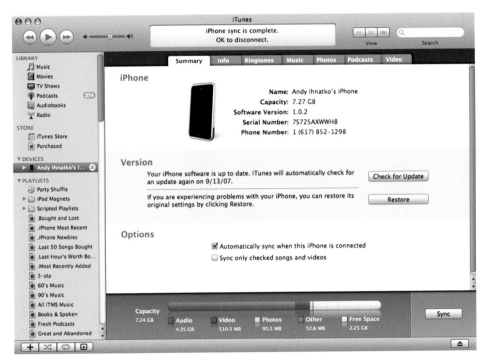

Figure 1-5
The iPhone Options window

or ...) library should be copied to your iPhone (see Figure 1-6).

Take this moment to observe the All Songs and Playlists Option. Click on this and your iPhone will contain all of the music in your library. Take a gooooood long look at it.

Ha ha! Yes, we all enjoyed a good laugh over that one. Most likely, unless you've only had your computer for 40 minutes, you already have way more music and video on your machine than you have free space on your iPhone. That's why iTunes allows you to narrow down the library to an easily managed subset of playlists.

Each pane of the iPhone Options window is a little different and addresses the unique-ities of that media. Video files tend to be humongous in their own right. An iPhone can handle a thousand songs, but a half-dozen movies can easily max the thing out. The Video tab lets you select individual shows or movies in addition to managing your content via playlists.

So that's the end of our first day of school. And now you see why we have all your little desks facing *me* instead of each other. This way, when the bell rings and you all flee into the hallways to whip out your phones and check in with Facebook, you can tell each other that this class was so *lame,* that you *totally* knew everything that Mr. Ihnatko discussed, that this is all so *easy.*

Meanwhile I'm the only one who saw the look on your face when I explained something elemental, and watched your eyes and ears go into full spread-spectrum capture

Figure 1-6
Moving tunes from desktop to hiptop

mode. Funny, none of your *friends* seemed like they were learning something new. I bet they'd be really amused if they knew that you've had an iPhone all this time and didn't know how synchs worked.

To put it more simply: Those Hostess cupcakes your mom puts in your lunch come two to a pack. Send one my way from time to time and nobody ever needs to know about this. *Capice?*

How To Make 8 Gigabytes Seem Like 80

The Skim

Stretching Storage with Smart Playlists ◼ The Rating Game

It's been getting increasingly more seemly and decreasingly less un-so with each passing week, but in the days between Apple's announcement of the iPhone and the day it actually shipped the thing, a certain class of people simply would *not* shut up about the fact that the iPhone doesn't have a hard drive.

"It doesn't have a hard drive," they would, in fact, say. "For $599" — the original price of the thing — "by golly, you should get a hard drive."

I'm not unsympathetic. I'm a frugal sort, and I believe that for $599 you should also get four all-weather radials, a leather interior, and air conditioning. But the iPhone is what it is. It is *not* a cheap $49 phone with only eight buttons that forces you to hold it upside down every time you need to dial a 9 or a 7.

Besides, 8 gigabytes (or even 4, if you own one of the first iPhones sold) is plenty of storage for a smartphone, if you use it properly. Even if you have an iPod Touch with 16 gigs, there's always a way to manage that storage better.

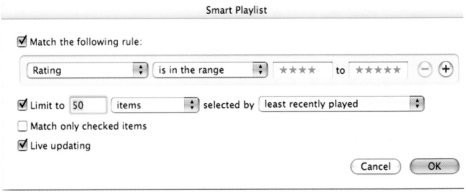

Figure 2-1
Keeping content fresh automatically, thanks to smart playlists

STRETCHING STORAGE WITH SMART PLAYLISTS

I have three different music players. I have about 300 gigabytes of media in my desktop iTunes library. My iPod has its 40-gig drive packed to the gills. And then I have my 8-gig iPhone. And yet when it comes to a simple question of the breadth of content, the listening experience with the iPhone is just about the same as what I enjoy with any other music player.

The reason for this is simple: Practically all the content on my iPhone is managed with smart playlists. Instead of assembling fixed lists of music and video, I have merely described the *kind* of stuff that iTunes should maintain on my phone at all times, and I allow the app to keep adjusting iPhone's content as time goes by. So although my iPhone only has 8 gigabytes of storage, the end effect is that iTunes is projecting a constantly moving 8-gig window of content from a media library that's 40 times larger.

I mean, think about it: It would take me about a month of nonstop listening to go through all the stuff on my iPhone. Which is nice, if you have the sort of job where you can take that much time off for personal projects, but I rarely go more than, say, two days before I dock my iPhone back to my computer. Every synch is another chance for iTunes to close the curtains and make sure there's a whole new scene in place by the time the curtains upon on the next act.

Figure 2-1 shows you a typical example of one of these playlists.

As you can see, it's dead-simple. The key is that bit at the bottom: Limit to 50 Items Selected By Least Recently Played. Both your iPhone and iTunes keep track of which tracks and videos you've played and when. If you go out for the day and listen to two hours' music, the next time iTunes sees that iPhone it'll note which ones you've heard and will delete 'em all from that smart playlist. Then, iTunes will replace them all with the tracks that you haven't played in, like, the longest time.

No, *actually* the longest time. iTunes will keep digging through your library, looking for lost treasures from your library.

That criterion is also useful when you set it to maintain a playlist of your library's freshest content.

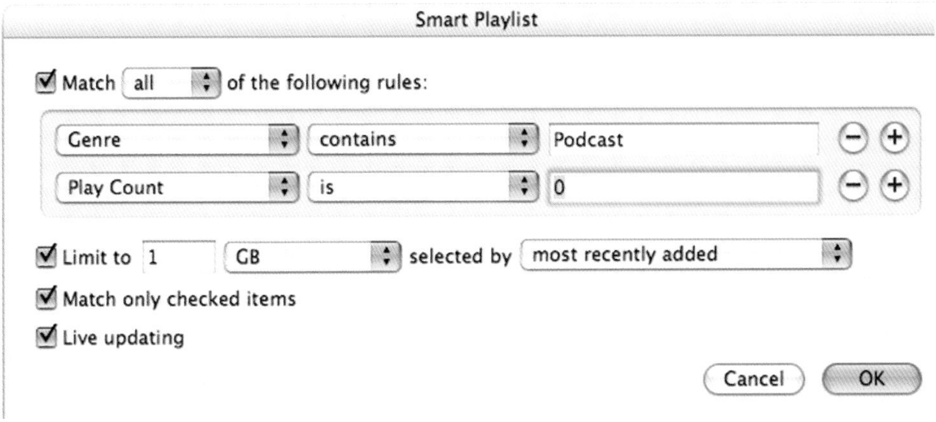

Figure 2-2
My daily dose of podcasts

iTunes is particularly good at maintaining a playlist of new podcasts (see Figure 2-2). It just looks for tracks whose genre is Podcast and chooses the recently added gigabytes' worth from among the podcasts I haven't heard yet.

The only slightly tricky bit is combining Most Recent with Unheard. Least Recently Played is one of the options in the selection criteria, but you can't select both options at once. Hence that extra line, specifying that the playlist should only select tracks that have been played 0 times.

I've subscribed to dozens of podcasts and so, some days, iTunes downloads more than 200 megabytes of daily news and entertainment. It becomes overwhelming; you quickly appreciate that you don't so much want to listen to *all* your new podcasts as they come in so much as you merely want to have quick access to the freshest content. This playlist puts a premium on the newest podcasts, and if there's something I've already heard, it's automatically eliminated.

So while I do have one manual playlist

labeled Must-Haves — for those perennial albums and videos that I always want to have handy — everything else is selected and synched to my phone automatically. I have about a dozen smart playlists covering every genre and situation. I always have 4 gigs of music I haven't heard in eons: 500 megs of jazz, 1 gig of classical, 1.5 gigs of rock, and a

TIP

The second big boon of a podcast playlist is that I can just push Play and all my new podcasts play one after the other. It's nice that the iPhone automatically arranges all its podcasts under its own special button, but as soon as it reaches the end of a three-minute segment of KRCW's *Martini Shot*, it stops dead, ignorant of the fact that I still have an hour drive ahead of me and Kevin Smith's *SmodCast* would fit that gap quite nicely.

15

TIDBIT

I have nothing against Neil Diamond or his fine catalogue of hit music. I made a Neil Diamond joke in print once and my big sister made the mistake of complaining about it, which of course, triggered a genetic response in a little brother to automatically want to do something to annoy an elder sister. That said, Neil Diamond fans, you really do have to finally confront the fact that *The Jazz Singer* was a wretched, wretched movie.

combined 500 gigs of country and bluegrass.

THE RATING GAME

Each track in your library can be rated (from zero to five stars), and that's an obviously powerful tool when trying to build smart playlists that choose music for you. The more tracks you rate, the better your smart playlists can become at choosing your favorite music.

But most people never get around to ratings, even though it's pretty easy. In iTunes, you just click the mouse in the Rating column next to the track, and assign it from 1 to 5 stars. Or, right-click the track's name to bring up the track's contextual menu (Mac owners can bring it up by holding down the Control key while clicking) and choose a rating via the Rating submenu.

You can even assign ratings right on your iPhone or iPod Touch. Just tap the album art twice while the track is playing, and then illuminate the appropriate number of stars with a second tap.

But it's a pain to go through all that for hundreds or even thousands or tens of thousands of tracks. But a smart playlist can actually automate the entire action, as Figure 2-3 shows.

The smart playlist in Figure 2-3 hunts for rock music that I haven't gotten around to rating. If I get in the habit of listening to this playlist as I take my morning constitutional and applying a rating to each tune as I hear it, I'll eventually get every last one of my rock tracks duly starred.

It's like dog training: There's a positive reward for taking a moment to tap the screen and register my opinion. Because this is the only playlist I listen to for the whole hour, and the *only* way to finally get that one Neil Diamond song *off* my iPhone is to assign it its one, lonely, and inevitable star so that iTunes will replace it with something that I *didn't* buy as a joke.

I set up that "Unrated Music" smart playlist on my iPhone and made it my usual playlist. It really didn't take long before I'd tagged thousands of tracks. I'm still barely a third of the way toward rating my entire library, but I'm already reaping huge rewards: There are times during a long ride when you want to be challenged with obscure tracks that shine a light on your preconceptions about art. But then there are those times when you just want to pump your fist in the air and yell, "She LOVES youuuu, yeahhh, Yeahhh, YEAHH, *YEAHHHHH!!!!*"

You can't really make that happen without having some ratings in your library.

So honestly, I can't say that I've had any complaints whatsoever about the lack of a hard drive in my iPhone, or the lack of a card slot (which is something you find in most smartphones).

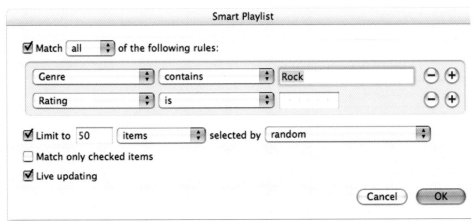

Figure 2-3
Hey, now you're a rock star! Or you will be, after using this smart playlist.

"Turn out your pockets," I said to one complainer. He'd really pushed me too far.

"What?"

"Right now. All of them. Let's see *everything* you have in your pockets. Because if the fact that the iPhone doesn't have a slot for additional storage card really *is* a total deal breaker for you, then you absolutely *must* be carrying more than 8 gigs of memory cards on you. If you aren't, then you're talking through your hat. And if you *are*, do you *really* prefer swapping cards three times in order to listen to *Quadrophenia* all the way through?

PART II

The Real World

Ripping CDs

The Skim

I promise you it's true: I held an actual CD in my hands. Just last week, in fact.

It was a little freaky. Kind of like that point in the guided tour of a zoo where you get to touch a boa constrictor. It's a little colder and stickier than you thought it was. I mean, I didn't freak out or anything, but still it was an exciting enough moment that I couldn't stop talking about for days afterward.

("And there was a little *book* inside it! On paper and everything! With pictures and lyrics. And Bono had, like, a *lot* of things to say about the situation in Costa Rica, but the text was teensy-tiny so I'm not really sure precisely what the trouble is down there. It still made me want to send the guy a lot of money, though.")

A whole generation is growing up without every having had to remove the shrinkwrap and those sticky strips from the edges of a brand-new CD. So if they're angry, resentful, violent, and despondent over the ability of a remorseful corporation to inflict wanton distress and suffering upon an innocent populace, then they'll need to find a new scapegoat.

For all the benefits of buying music online and downloading it via podcast and directly from bands' Web sites, the CD still offers practical advantages over any other method. I shall start off by mentioning that

Figure 3-1
Opening a CD in iTunes

at this writing, one and only one Stan Freberg track is available from the iTunes Store. I suppose there might be others, but really, do they matter?

iTunes makes it dead-simple to convert CDs into digital music files. But there are subtleties that you ought to know about, particularly before you eye the 700 discs in your collection and begin a heroic month-long ripping campaign.

IMPORTING MUSIC CDS

Okey-doke. Just stick a CD in the drive and after your machine has taken a moment to comprehend that it now has to deal with a copy of Howard Jones's *Greatest Hits*, iTunes opens the CD for playback and presents

you with a list of tracks (see Figure 3-1) and (unless little Norbert has unchecked this option) asks if you want to import the CD.

If you push iTunes's Play button, it'll play these tracks straight off the CD, but we're living in the exciting Push-Button World of Tomorrow, not the leaden gaslight-and-spats era of the mid-Nineties: We want to make music files.

Turning all those tracks into digital music files is a complicated process consisting of:

1. Push the button marked Import CD, found in the lower-right corner of the iTunes window (see Figure 3-2).

2. (optional) Go to the kitchen and microwave a Hot Pocket or something while the tracks are converted to music files and added to your iTunes library.

Because, honestly, that's all there is to it. I desperately wanted only one step, so I wantonly chose to gloss over the fact that if there are any tracks on this disc that you don't want, you just click the checkbox next to the tracks' names. I mean, on the off-chance that the artists who created this CD failed to ensure that every single track was a timeless classic.

As you enjoy your Hot Pocket, you might pass the time by noting some of the things that are going on in the window (see Figure 3-3):

Figure 3-2
The Import button, a.k.a. All You Need To Know

Figure 3-3
The rip-in-progress

Figure 3-4
Spitting out the disc

- The window's status display shows you which track is currently being imported, how far along the process has come, and, if you like to brag about how fast your computer is, the speed of the rip. Here, iTunes is pleased to report that it's converting the track thirteen times faster than it'd take to play it. I'm your friend, so I'll take this moment to quietly tell you that *nobody* is impressed with the speed of your new computer. Honest. They're feigning interest. Your friends used to think this sort of behavior was amusing, but now they can no longer sit by and watch you strike out time and time again talking about your new laptop, your hybrid car, the new watch you bought for marathon training, etc. "The best way to talk is to *listen*," they urge you. I concur heartily. They're not trying to embarrass you. They just don't want you to be so terribly *lonely*, that's all.

- Next to the numbers on the left side of the track list are little green checkmark icons that represent completed tracks, an orange one next to the track that's being ripped right now, and colorful expanses of absolutely nothing next to

those tracks yet to be processed, glistening with the promise of digital files yet to come.

- Check the tiny X button on the right side of iTunes's status display to abort the rip-in-progress only if you want to cancel all the tracks due to be ripped.

- iTunes will start playing the ripped tracks as soon as the first one is complete unless you've turned that particular feature off in iTunes's Preferences panel. Click the Stop button to knock that off.

After iTunes has finished ripping the disc, you can eject it from your computer by clicking the little Eject button next to the CD's name in the Devices list on the left side of the iTunes window (see Figure 3-4), the big Eject button in the lower-right corner of the iTunes window, or by pressing the Eject button on your keyboard or on your CD drive.

My job as an instructionalist writer is 95 percent done. Nothin' left for me to do here

TIDBIT

Ripping your first disc is simple. It's the remaining 992 in your collection that are going to sting. Fortunately, there are lots of services out there that will rip all your CDs *for* you. You ship 'em the discs, they ship 'em all back accompanied by a few DVDs filled with iTunes-compatible music files. These services are popping up all over the place, but if you want to check out pricing, RipTopia (www.riptopia.com) and MusicShifter (www.musicshifter.com) are good places to start.

but clear up a few trims and ends, most of which orbit the theme of "Why Did This Go Wretchedly Wrong?"

TROUBLESHOOTING

But this world is a vale of tears, and even in a simple, flawless, and foolproof process like iTunes CD ripping, a little rain must fall, viz:

The Disc Didn't Appear in iTunes

If the disc doesn't show up in iTunes, there are usually two possible answers:

■ The disc is way too baffed-up for your CD drive to recognize. I mean, for heaven's sake, man: You felt your chair roll over it *twice* before you picked it up. That's going to cost you a new copy of *Rubber Soul*, my friend.

■ The disc isn't an audio CD.

"Not an audio CD," eh? Interesting. Usually, this means that the publisher chose to save you a little time by burning a CD-R or

a DVD-R of digital music files. Open the disc in Windows Explorer or the Mac OS Finder and see what files are there. If it's loaded with .mp3 or .aac or other music-ish filename extensions, you can just drag those files straight into the iTunes window and they'll be added to your music library without any further ado.

Sometimes, though — and if you listen carefully, you can hear my teeth grinding as I type these words — it's because the CD has been intentionally corrupted by the publisher. Which brings us to …

"Copy-Prevented" Discs

And I put those words in quotes because it's nonsense. If you legally purchased a CD, then you have the right to rip its tracks into digital music files. Period. It a right that's specifically included in U.S. copyright law. Moreover, the music industry has tried time and time again to weaken this provision or specify cases in which it doesn't matter, and time and time again, the courts have smacked them in their collective nose with a rolled-up newspaper and told them to sleep outside tonight.

So the recording industry's response to these defeats has been to flirt with the idea of "corrupting" some of their most popular titles just enough so that computers don't recognize them as audio CDs.

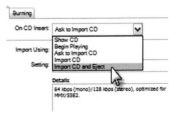

Figure 3-5
Turning your computer into a ripping station

Which is in itself a fool's errand; the CD standard is called a standard for a good reason. Because, um, when it fails to conform to the standard, it no longer meets the standard. (To wit: There's now a good chance that this disc won't play in a car CD changer, or the CD boom box that you bought a few years ago, or any audio CD player anywhere.)

These crippled discs are rare — I think even the music industry understands that these schemes don't really work, and only result in consumer backlash — but all the same, *why* did they ever go to all this trouble?

I don't know. I've never drunk a pint of raw ether, so I lack the ability to process thoughts in quite the same way as a music company executive. "To prevent piracy" is the usual smokescreen, but in truth the goal is to assert more control over what you can do with the music that you own. I bought one copy of The Who's *Who's Next* fifteen years ago, and because I never lost or ruined it, and I've converted the disc to crisp, perfect digital files, it's likely that I'll never buy another copy again. This presents A Problem for the record industry.

Onward.

There are limits to how angry I can get about copy-protected CDs because none of the systems that are currently in play actually work. Here's how to get around nearly any copy-protection scheme:

If you're a Windows user:

1. Hold down the Shift key while inserting the CD.

And you're done. Most of these anti-copying schemes work by sticking an invisible piece of Windows software that runs automatically when Windows mounts the CD. The sole purpose of this app is to prevent the disc's contents from being ripped. But

> **TIP**
>
> If you're settling down to rip dozens or hundreds of discs instead of a handful, iTunes has a hidden feature to speed things along. To do so, choose Edit ▶ Preference in Windows and iTunes ▶ Preferences on the Mac. Click the Advanced tab, and then click the Importing subtab (see Figure 3-5).
>
> Click the On CD Insert pop-up menu and you'll reveal a frisky item named Import Songs And Eject. It's tailor-made for processing CDs in bulk: Whenever it sees a disc, it rips all the tracks and then spits it out again, hungry for more.
>
> You can rip a 1,000-CD collection with little visible effort by merely keeping a stack of discs near the computer and getting in the habit of sticking a new disc in there whenever a ripped disc is sticking out of the drive.

holding down the Shift key tells Windows to ignore any auto-run software on the disc.

You should also refuse to install any "bonus" software included on the disc. Often, the "special video footage" or the "special access to an exclusive Web site" offer is actually a Trojan horse: The CD will also install a permanent piece of software on your PC that will eternally look out for CDs published by that same company and prevent you from ripping its tracks into your music library.

If you're a Mac user, the solution is simpler still:

…

Yeah, you don't have to do anything at all.

Figure 3-6
The untitled symphony

These copy-prevention schemes are almost always keyed to work on Windows computers only. Macs will mount the disc and rip its tracks without any complaint.

I hate to keep going on and on about this (oh, what a *lie,* Ihnatko!), but I can't help myself. The whole point of introducing all this malicious spyware and corrupting discs so that they won't play on "real" CD players was (allegedly) to prevent these tracks from winding up on the Internet. Does the recording industry believe that Mac users don't have access to the Internet, and they're all

so noble and pure that none of them would ever illegally post a song on a file-sharing service? So the companies have inconvenienced thousands of paying customers, with absolutely no benefit. Idiots!

All the Tracks Are Untitled

Magically, iTunes fills in the title of the CD and the names of artists on each track for you. This particular mojo is powered by a massive online database containing info about very nearly (accent on "very nearly") every CD ever made. If you have an Internet

Figure 3-7
Let iTunes's fingers do the typing.

connection, iTunes automatically connects to the database, asks, "Have you ever heard of this CD before?", and grabs the info it needs.

If something goes wrong, you'll see the unhappy state of affairs represented by Figure 3-6.

If you didn't have an Internet connection available when you ripped the disc, don't sweat it. The next time you're Net-studly, select those tracks and then choose Advanced
♦ Get CD Track Names (see Figure 3-7).

It's possible, however, that you are the first human on this planet to ever purchase and rip this specific CD. In which case the database doesn't *have* any album, artist, or track info on file. You'll have to add that stuff yourself. Here's how:

1. Select the first track in the album.
2. In iTunes, choose File ♦ Get Info.
3. Click on the window's Info tab. You'll be presented with the little form you

see in Figure 3-8. Laboriously copy all that info from the back of the CD. When you finish one track, click the Next button to move on to the next track.

If you select more than one track before choosing Get Info, iTunes will (after a curt warning that this might be a bad idea) allow you to edit the info for all those tracks at once. The album, year, genre, and maybe even the artist and composer won't change from track to track, so it's a good way to save some time. But you're going to want to dismiss that window and then edit each track individually to add the specific track titles.

And this is your reward for supporting struggling independent artists. Because honestly, the only CDs that aren't in the Gracenote CDDB — where iTunes gets all its CD info — are coffee-shop performers who self-produce CDs in the dozens or hundreds at best. Every commercial CD is already there, no matter how bizarre. To produce Figure 3-6, I dug out my copy of *The Beatles on Panpipes,* a gag gift I bought for a Beatles fan pal and then didn't have the

TROUBLE

Just to demonstrate what sort of egg-sucking weasels we're dealing with here:

One major music publisher hid a *major* piece of spyware on all its major releases. Not only did it prevent you from copying tracks but it also kept tabs on your listening habits.

And the kicker: It was

installed using a technique that made the software (a) difficult to detect, (b) almost impossible to remove without destroying your whole system, and (c) open a major hole in the security of your PC.

Idiots! They deserve to go through life in itchy underwear. And to have something heavy dropped

on them from a great height.

Naturally, hackers discovered this and started to deploy malicious software of their own, designed to exploit the gaping hole created by the record company's spyware. Just desserts, I tell you!

courage to actually give him. But no, a disc of panpipe-based Beatles covers had already been processed and added to the database.

(Stuck for a solution, I eventually realized that I could accomplish what I wanted if I simply turned off my notebook's Wi-Fi for a few minutes. Me am Number 1 clever technology writer of all.)

After you've finished all that work, you *could* demonstrate that you're a responsible and contributing member of society by selecting the tracks and choosing Advanced ▶ Submit CD Track Names.

This will update the CDDB with the info you've just added to iTunes, and potentially the rest of the world will benefit from your labors, in perpetuity.

Not the best legacy that you can leave, but it's more than some people will ever contribute, I suppose.

CHOOSING A MUSIC FORMAT

There. That's better. We've come this far and we've only used a handful of acronyms. But they're all friendly and familiar ones: CD, PC, even LP, for the love of Mike.

Take a deep breath, because it's time to knock you down and pummel you with MP3, AAC, VBR, and other key players in the Obfuscation Hit Parade.

When you convert CD tracks into music files, there are a few different goals you want to achieve with the results:

▶ **You want the tracks to sound good**. We shall refer to this as the "Duh" Imperative.

▶ **You want files that don't take up a whole lot of space**. Because you have a limited amount of space on your iPhone, and if iTunes is creating music files that are twice as big as they need to be, then your iPhone or iPod Touch can only hold half as many tracks as it should.

▶ **You don't want to go through this bloody mess of ripping dozens, if not hundreds, of CDs all over again for any reason**. A subtler point, this, but nonetheless it's something you ought to consider. You are a luminous being, one of the Beloveds of the Universe, my child; your destiny is a long one and unless you're reading this book while driving a car, it's likely that you're going to be on this planet for many years to come.

"But wait," you're now thinking, after fully digesting the "Beloved of the Universe" line.

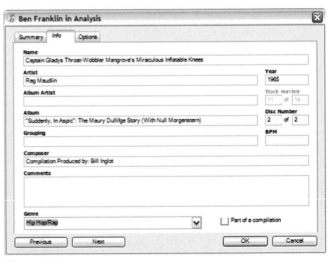

Figure 3-8

Pin the info on the track list, one by one.

"That means I really *shouldn't* go get the space-ship from *Battlestar Galactica* tattooed across my back, because although *right now* I think it's the most awesome show ever, and really sums up my outlook and philosophy of life, maybe I'll feel differently ten years from now!" Indeed it does. That's not where I was going with that, but I'm glad that you're gleaning bits of incidental wisdom from this book.

So before you rip that Strokes CD, stop and picture yourself six months from now, when you've bought a doohickey that lets you plug your iPod Touch into your big home stereo system; or a year from now, when you have an AppleTV or some other box that can wirelessly transmit music from your computer to speakers anywhere in the house; or an iPhone, of course.

If you make the right choices today, you can create music files that will play on your iPhone or iPod Touch (good) and in iTunes (fab), but also nearly any sort of digital audio device or accessory that you might put your hands on in the next five or ten years. It'll come down to:

- **File format**. You can't stick an eight-track into a CD drive, and not all devices and software can play every conceivable music file format. You want iTunes to use a file format that will work on the greatest range of stuff.
- **Sound quality**. "Hey, this file sounds great" is a relative term. Bruce Vilanch humming the score from *The Magnificent Seven* would sound great, too, through those crappy white earbuds that came with the iPhone and iPod Touch. iTunes will always make certain sacrifices and tradeoffs when converting a CD track into a music file, and often they're only apparent when you listen through a halfway decent set of home speakers. And look, if you've ripped a large CD collection into iTunes, one of the first things you want to do is enjoy your music collection through your stereo. That's a bad time to discover that iTunes ripped all your tracks at the Bruce Vilanch setting.

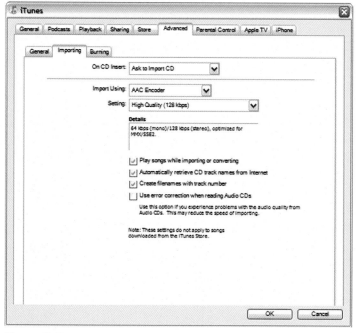

Figure 3-9
Modifying iTunes's default settings for ripping music

Figure 3-10
iTunes's custom quality settings

The Settings That I Think You Ought to Use

I'm betting that you're interested more in immediate gratification than technical detail. So let's lead off with the tweaks I think you ought to make to iTunes's default music-ripping settings. You can access these settings by choosing Edit ▶ Preferences in Windows and iTunes ▶ Preferences on the Macintosh. Click the Advanced tab, and then click the Importing tab below (see Figure 3-9).

In the Import Using pop-up menu, stick with the default choice of AAC Encoder.

The sound quality setting is a slightly more complicated issue. There's a quickie menu labeled Setting but to get at the good stuff, you'll need to select Custom from the bottom of that menu (see Figure 3-10).

Figure 3-7 shows three pop-up menus and two different options. You only want to change the Stereo Bit Rate. By default, it's set at 128Kbps. Change it to 192.

There it is: Rip all your tracks to the AAC file format, using a sample rate of 192Kbps. I think that's the sweet spot that gives you terrific-sounding files that will play on a huge variety of devices but won't choke the capacity of your iPhone.

Now let's get into a deeper explanation.

File Formats

iTunes can rip music into a buttload of different formats:

- **MP3.** "MP3" is the Band-Aid of digital music. It means one format, specifically, but because it was the first really popular digital music format released, it became a huge success. The world tends to use the word "MP3" specifically when it really is just referring to digital music files in general. And here you see the big advantage of MP3: Practically every piece of software and any piece of hardware anywhere created by anybody who breathes the human mixture of oxygen, carbon dioxide, and nitrogen gases can handle an MP3 file, whether it's a music player on a cell phone or a piece of software that lets you edit your home movies and create your own soundtracks.

- **AAC.** The Advanced Audio Coding format was created after digital music took off and is the collective answer to the question "How can we make MP3 suck less?" Which is not to say that MP3 *sucks.* But it has a pretty shallow bag of tricks. The industry developed AAC a few years later and with a few years of additional experience in compressing music. The upshot is that AAC files sound better than MP3s And they take up less space. Well, generally speaking, that is. Keep in mind that the wonks out there absolutely insist they can hear the difference between an LP and a CD. And there are ultra-ultra-wonks who claim that they can tell you what metal your speaker wires are made from. If you're at a party, you're meant to be dancing, not scrutinizing the music for time resolution and scale factor artifacts. You can indeed make an MP3 that sounds as good as an AAC file, but it'll still probably take up more space.

☑ **AIFF and Apple Lossless**. I've grouped these together because they fill the same function: To create the most perfect copy of the original CD track possible. Absolutely no sacrifices whatsoever will be made in the name of quality. This is a *good* thing if you're truly trying to archive your CDs permanently, creating a library of "masters" that you can burn duplicates from for years to come. This is a *bad* thing if you're truly trying to get more than, say, three songs to fit on your iPhone at once. Sacrifices have to be made *somewhere,* and if you're not willing to sacrifice sound quality you're going to have to sacrifice file size to the max.

☑ **WAV**. The iPhone and iPod Touch support this format and so I suppose I'm begrudgingly required to report that yes, iTunes can rip to this format, too. But why on *earth* would you want to? WAV files are really big, they sound like a used coffee filter, and they're really only used by music producers who haven't bought new recording and mixing software in the past five years. Avoid.

Your choice comes down to just AAC and MP3, and MP3's sole advantage is that it's a bit more widely supported. But it's a negligible advantage and even that minor gap continues to narrow. As a beloved industry columnist, I have dozens of devices in my office that play digital music files, and the only thing I have that can play MP3s but not AAC files is a bizarre wristwatch music player that I got as a party favor.

Sound Quality

The Sound Quality setting in iTunes is really the bit rate that iTunes uses when it converts a track into a music file. A higher bit rate translates into more detail. A happy face is a picture of your Uncle Sid ripped at the lowest possible bit rate. A moderate bit rate is a cartoon that looks like him. Higher, and it's a drawing that looks *exactly* like him. An image of Sid at the highest possible bit rate is a photo.

When you set the bit rate, you're telling iTunes, "Here's how much detail you can put into every second of the music file." As you might have guessed, though, when you increase the bit rate, all that extra detail amounts to a larger file. A track that was ripped with iTunes's default 128Kbps bit rate won't sound as good as the same track ripped at 256Kbps, but it'll take up half as much space on your iPhone and leave room for more music.

Bit rates are frustrating because they're so subjective. A drop in detail that one listener won't even notice will render a song unlistenable by another. And some songs are practically bulletproof. You can compress them down to nearly nothing without inflicting any damage.

I chose 192Kbps because it's a good compromise. Using the AAC format, 128Kbps is just fine for damned-near every piece of music you throw at it. But if you rip a wide range of music styles (rock, folk, classical, skate-metal, …) and you listen to enough music, you will inevitably be listening to (probably) a quiet piece played on acoustic instruments, and you'll realize that on *this* track and in *this* passage, a rich, thready violin sounds a bit … well, I dunno, mushy? I'd come up with a better word for it but the defect has already gone away, apparently, and it didn't really last long enough for me to focus in on it.

It's a problem of philosophy. You're going to be ripping all your music into iTunes. If you're unhappy with the sound quality later on, there's nothing you can do about it except rip it all over again at a higher setting. I have over two terabytes of storage on my Mac, and my iPhone can hold more music than I can possibly listen to in a whole month. I'm willing to put up with slightly larger music files if it means that a violin always sounds like a violin.

Because we're ripping with an iPhone or iPod Touch in mind — devices that don't have a beefy hard drive — be flexible. I do think it's worth it to rip music at a higher bit rate, but if you're ripping a book on tape, drop the bit rate down to 96Kbps or even lower. It could be the difference between a three-hour file fitting on your device along with your other tracks and having to leave it home. F. Murray Abraham has a fine voice and you don't need to hear it at maximum quality to follow all the plot points of the latest Danielle Steele bodice-ripper.

So, before you rip that *particular* disc, open the import preferences and choose Spoken Podcast from the Setting pop-up menu. Just remember to restore iTunes to its previous bit-rate settings when you're finished — after all, these settings will apply to every track you rip.

One other import setting that's worth mentioning: Variable Bit Rate Encoding, a.k.a. VBR. This is a keen idea in which instead of sticking with the same bit rate every single second, iTunes can dial it down whenever it determines that you won't be able to hear the difference. Five seconds of

silence is five seconds of silence, whether it's being ripped at 256Kbps or 60Kbps, you know?

Selecting the Variable Bit Rate Encoding option can lead to smaller files. But I leave it unchecked (which is also iTunes's default) because (a) *some* third-party music players don't like VBR, and (b) although VBR does indeed produce smaller files, it's not a dramatic enough improvement to make (a) worthwhile.

Regard me as a member of the Sadder-But-Wiser Club. The year I added my first truly humongous drive to my desktop was the year I determined to finally rip every last track of every last CD I owned into iTunes. Nearly 800 in all.

Using that Import Songs And Eject setting that I told you about earlier, I set up a laptop near the door to my office and kept a bin of CDs underneath. For a whole month, every time I went into the office for any reason whatsoever, I would remove a "done" CD from the drive and replace it with a fresh one from the bin. At the end, the drive held a majestic 14,000 songs.

And then I had to do them all over again. Because I got this great little wireless box that streamed music files from iTunes anywhere in the house. But it didn't like the file format I chose, and it gakked all over the VBR setting as well.

Which is why my personal library has been ripped even more conservatively than I've advised you guys. Maximum possible bit rate, maximum possible compatibility. I've ripped 14,000 songs twice now and if I have to do it a third time, dammit, it's going to be done by a trained monkey in a little uniform.

Ripping DVDs

The Skim

There are times when I am so relieved that I don't get to ask Apple's CEO any questions directly when he gives a big keynote address promoting the company's products and services.

"And the iTunes Store continues to be an immense success, quickly becoming the industry's largest seller of downloadable movies," Steve Jobs boasted in a recent keynote. "Why, at this moment, the store has more than *300* feature-length films available for download!"

Applause, applause. And then my hand would have gone up.

"Yes, Ihnatko, there at the back?"

"Thanks. Um, I just wanted to know why the devil *anybody* should be impressed with 300 downloadable movie titles? I mean, I *own* 300 commercial DVDs. Aren't there, like, over 100,000 movies available on DVD or something? And even if I *do* see a movie in the iTunes Store that I actually want well, it's hardly a bargain, is it? It's just two or three dollars less than what I could get the DVD for at Best Buy … and *that* comes with four hours of bonus material."

This is the point at which I'd have been thrown into a big sack and dragged from the building. Well, those are the chances that a man in my position (sitting cross-legged on a sofa with a wireless keyboard in my lap) must take if he's to uphold his mandate to his readers.

No, you *shouldn't* be impressed with mere hundreds of downloadable movies at the iTunes Store. You *shouldn't* be content with saving $4 off the cost of a $17 DVD that comes with bonus material, outtakes, commentary tracks, and all sorts of goodies that you don't get with the down-loaded version.

Not when there's a terrific tool for both PCs and Macs that can convert any DVD — whether commercial or burned on your home DVD recorder — to an iPhone-able movie file. *Double*-not, considering this tool is free, free, and dare I say free.

IS THIS LEGAL?

Oh, come now. Is following the system of laws that keeps our democracy in place *all* that you care about?

It is?

Good. Just checking. My iPhone currently has three movies on it, and none of them are available for legal download anywhere. This leads some people to conclude that I in fact downloaded them *illegally*, from any one of hundreds of naughty file-sharing sites.

(Um, "naughty" meaning "the sites encourage and allow people to steal copy-righted movies," not "the sites feature lots of poorly shot videos of pizza deliverymen and lonely stewardesses.)

Yes, this is legal. It's easy to steal movies from various file-sharing services and this book *is* about filling your iPhone or iPod Touch to capacity, but I won't explain how to use those services. And I'll tell you why: It's just plain wrong. No sarcasm, jokes, or subtle winks here. If you want it, you have to have the legal right to use it. In the case of movies, that means either buying the DVD at the store or recording it off cable. (And you *are* paying for cable, right?)

Once you've obtained a legal copy of the movie (or TV show, or cartoon, or …), you have every right to make a copy that you can play on your iPhone or iPod. U.S. copyright law outlines several scenarios under which you can duplicate copyrighted material, and it's right there in black and white: If you own it, you can copy it from one medium (such as a DVD) to another (such as a movie file) for your personal use. So it's perfectly legal.

Pretty much.

As far as anyone can tell.

The only problem is that there's this *other* bit of the law, added in the 1990s, which says that if a publisher has put some sort of mojo on the recording to prevent copying, then it's illegal to break that copy protection. So on the one hand, the law says you have every right to copy that movie; on the other hand, it says that you're not really allowed to *exercise* that right if the publisher doesn't want you to.

So which part of the law wins? We dunno. A law hasn't received its official bar mitzvah until it's been tested in courts, and either upheld or overturned. Naturally, the very last thing the recording industry wants is for a judge to explicitly underscore consum-ers' rights to copy movies regardless of the publisher's desire, so they've never dared do anything about any DVD copying done at the consumer level.

Instead, the recording industry has made it *extremely* difficult for a company to sell software that breaks the encryption on com-mercial discs. But where there's a will — or a world of people with empty iPhones, iPods, and other video players — there's a way.

RIPPING WITH HANDBRAKE

The great friend to the freedom-loving proletariat is a free app, available for both

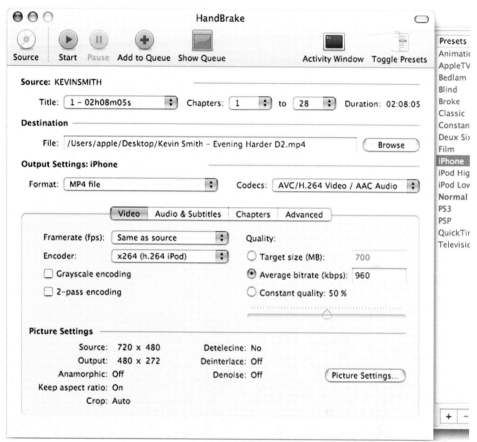

Figure 4-1
HandBrake: the handy ecumenical app that copies DVDs

Windows *and* the Mac OS, known as Hand-Brake (Figure 4-1 shows the Mac edition).

It's nearly impossible for the movie industry to shut this app down (as it has done so successfully with so many other such apps) because — and get this — no one company owns it or profits from it. It's "open source" software, which means that it's built, maintained, updated, and distributed by a worldwide community of software developers. You might as well try to sue the stink off a pig farm; it's everywhere and nowhere, so there's

no real target.

You can download a copy of HandBrake for either Windows or Mac from the app's official site: http://handbrake.m0k.org.

Both versions share the same user interface, mostly. And they *very nearly* share all the same features. The Windows version is missing just one teensy (but I think you'll agree, vital) feature: the ability to convert commercial copy-protected DVDs in addition to the ones you burn at home.

Mac users, take a smoke break or something. Me and the Windows people need to figure out a way around this.

DECRYPTING WITH ANYDVD

All righty. Good news, sensation-seekers, because SlySoft (www.slysoft.com) has come to the rescue with a rather simple and awesome little app: AnyDVD. It'll cost you fifty bucks (at this writing) but it's a magical app and it's well worth the dough.

AnyDVD does one thing. It does it well, and it does it invisibly: It breaks the copy protection on commercial DVDs and bamboozles Windows into thinking it's just an ordinary, plain-Jane disc.

For the sake of completeness, and to take advantage of the lovely color layout of this book, I'll go ahead and show you what Any-DVD looks like.

Figure 4-2 shows the window that comes up if you click on the little cartoon fox that AnyDVD puts in your system tray. But hon-estly, it's just there to satisfy your curiosity and to confirm that it's working. Whenever you insert a DVD, AnyDVD grabs it before Windows or any other app ever sees it. It silently performs the mojo required to break the copy protection on the disc, and *then* it presents it to the operating system.

From that point onward, any time any app makes a request for some of the data on the DVD, that request is handled by AnyDVD. It decrypts the data and passes it along to the app that wanted it, without the app's knowledge that anything unusual had taken place at all. As far as the app is concerned, it's as though Pixar decided to actually, you know, *trust* you by selling you a copy of *The Incredibles* without copy protection.

OKAY, BACK TO HANDBRAKE

Welcome back, Mac people. Why does HandBrake for Mac contain the magical DVD-unlocking mojo and not the Windows edition? Because there are, like, a jillion more Windows machines out there than Macs, so we Macoids sort of slipped past the movie industry's storm troopers. So don't get all smug there about your platform of choice, Mac people.

In any event, we're all now on the same page. We all have HandBrake running on our computers

Figure 4-2

SlySoft's AnyDVD tames even the most savagely copy-protected commercial DVD.

TROUBLE

I know that you're not here to feel sorry for me — though frankly, any pity you can throw my way is heartily appreciated — but it's probably worth pointing out how bloody difficult it is to write about DVD rippers that run on Windows. It's a nightmare, I tell you!

In the years I've been writing about this stuff, I've embraced and lost at least three different and terrific apps.

One by one, like the red-shirted crewmembers of the *USS Enterprise* who join Kirk, Spock, and the rest of the "name" cast on dangerous missions, these apps have been picked off by the movie industry's weasels.

SlySoft actually makes a lovely little app called CloneDVD that does every-thing that Hand-Brake does. But it costs $40 and I can't really count on them selling it a year from now.

Why? Because it's Ensign McDonnell. It's wearing a red shirt, and it's just been sent off to investigate that strange noise coming from that rock that looks like it has a mouth and teeth.

and it is capable of converting commercial discs. Figure 4-3 shows you the Windows version of HandBrake; I'll be using it for all the examples that follow.

Converting a DVD takes just four steps:

1. Point HandBrake at the DVD. You do this by clicking the Browse button and then either selecting the disc in the file browser or navigating directly to the VIDEO_TS folder on the disc.

2. Tell HandBrake that you'd like the app to prepare a video file that's opti-mized for the iPhone. In Windows, you do this by selecting iPhone from the Presets menu. On the Mac, you'll find the presets in the drawer on the right side of the window, which you can open by clicking the Toggle Presets button. HandBrake will choose all the settings that are appropriate for a video file playing on your iPhone. iPod Touch users should also use this set-ting, assuming they haven't thrown in a Touch preset by the time you read this.

3. Choose the content that you want to convert by choosing a selection from the Title pop-up menu. A disc's con-tent is chopped up into several differ-ent "titles" that you never see because you usually navigate through it from that bouncy menu on your TV. In real-ity, a DVD might have one title just for the main menu animation, a second for the actual movie, a third for a ver-sion of the movie with scenes restored from the director's first cut, that sort of thing. Usually the correct title just jumps right out at you. If you're con-verting *Terminator 2*, your eye's sort of drawn to that one title that claims to be 2 hours and 32 minutes long, as opposed to the one that runs for 33 seconds.

4. Choose a destination for the video file. Give it a good name. HandBrake will choose one for you based on how the title is defined by the disc, but *Apocalypse Now — Redux Edition* is

TIDBIT

One note about the Windows edition of HandBrake: It's what's called a ".Net" application. What that means to you is that you'll need to have Microsoft's free .Net 2.0 framework installed on your PC. Oh, a technical explanation of .Net 2.0? It's, er, a set of little software gremlins that helps .Net 2.0 apps like HandBrake run. It's likely that you already have .Net installed on your PC, but if HandBrake complains when you launch it, you can download .Net for free from Microsoft. The download URL is so big that it'd choke a giraffe so I'll point you to www.microsoft.com/downloads and tell you to type ".Net framework" into the Search box. The first hit returned will probably be ".Net Framework Version 2.0 Redistributable Package." That's the baby.

latest and greatest hardware: On my brand-new, just-released iMac, a two-hour movie is ready in just over an hour.

HandBrake will end the process by making a snarky comment about how long it took to finish the conversion. Pretend not to be annoyed and you're done: Just drag the file into your iTunes library and presto, it can be synched to your iPhone without any further ado.

The neat thing about HandBrake's iPhone setting is that it's truly one-stop shopping. All the decisions have been made for you and the only thing you really need to do is figure out whether you'd prefer to pace fitfully or fretfully while your computer works on the problem.

But it has plenty of little tweaks, options, and settings, proving once again that life is a banquet and that we have but to take our seats and dig in to two in particular.

First, if you're converting a DVD that contains a dozen episodes of a TV series, you'll want to know about HandBrake's Queue feature. Repeat all of the steps above verbatim, and click Add To Queue instead of the Start button (on the Mac) or Encode to Video button (in Windows). Select the next episode, give it a different name, and click the Add To Queue button. Repeat until you've added all the content you'd like to rip. When you click the Start or Encode to Video button, HandBrake will grind on each of these videos in turn, leaving you free to pursue those many humanitarian efforts that you've been putting off for way too long.

Second, HandBrake can include any audio track you want. If the movie has several audio tracks (a director's commentary, a foreign language track, etc.) you can select that track from HandBrake's Audio Settings panel

going to make more sense to you than ANOWR-99. But I suppose I shouldn't assume. Do whatever you want. You're an incorrigible movie pirate; you're a maverick who plays by your own rules! (Well, not really, but it's fun to pretend.)

And that's really it. If you're using Windows, click the Encode Video button. On the Mac, click Start.

And wait.

Lots.

If you have a 5,000-piece jigsaw puzzle, now's a good time to take it back to the store and buy a 10,000-piece one. If you have an older computer, converting a movie to a movie file can take as long as four times the running time of the actual film. So here's yet another reason to envy folks who own the

(in Windows) or Audio & Subtitles panel (on the Mac). The only trick is that it's up to you to figure out which track is which. The first audio track is always the plain-vanilla one, but if there are three additional ones you'll have to resort to a little bit of trial-and-error to figure out which one is the cast of *Reno: 911!* riffing on the movie in-character and which one is the cast commenting as themselves.

The fabby thing about HandBrake is that it always works. There's nothing tricky about it. In the years I've been ripping DVDs, the only one that hasn't worked is *The Shaw-shank Redemption*. And there's hardly any car crashes in that one at all, so hey, no great loss.

If the movie industry has taken such great pains to prevent you from copying DVDs, why is it so bloody easy?

Oh, you'll love this: Because they were way, *way* too secretive when they developed the encryption method.

The funny thing about encryption is that when you're developing a new method, secrecy is the very *last* thing you want. You

want to share your efforts with the cryptography community at every stage, have them peer at it from every conceivable angle. In short, you want people to try to break it early on, before you commit to this system and you've lost the ability to make it stronger.

But no, the same industry that thought that remaking the Oscar-winning *All the King's Men* was a good idea also thought that developing an encryption scheme behind closed doors would work gangbusters. And sure enough, within a year, weaknesses were found, published, and widely exploited.

If Wile E. Coyote had gone for his MBA instead of spending all that dough on Acme merchandise, then surely he'd be a high-

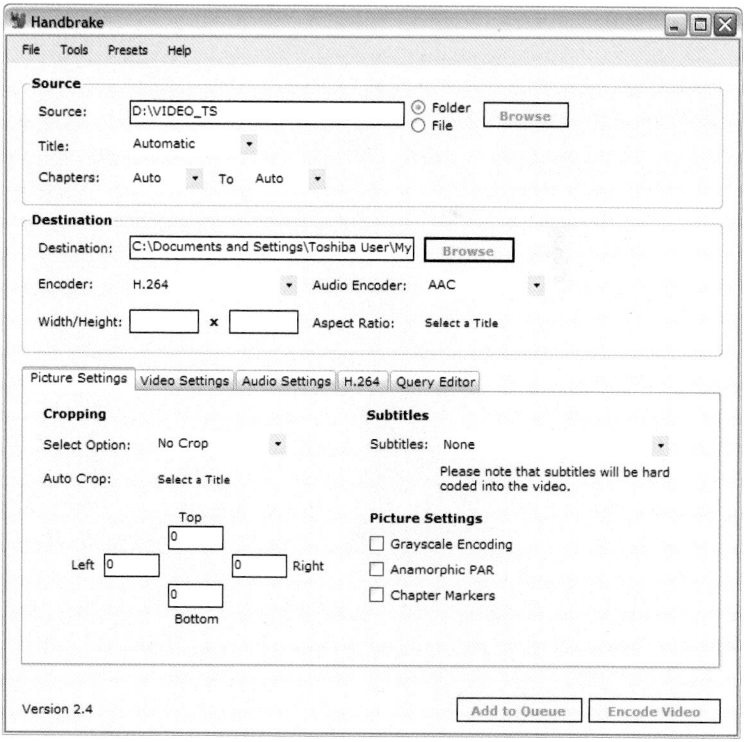

Figure 4-3
HandBrake for Windows

ranking executive with the Motion Picture Association of America.

Now if you'll excuse me, I have a four-hour train ride tomorrow, and HandBrake has just finished converting the original, *non-hideous* version of *All the King's Men*.

Old Home Video

The Skim

The Basic Idea ▪ The Hardware ▪ The Software

I have a VHS machine and a LaserDisc player in my office. In the grand cast of characters that is My Collection of Technology, they're Fredo Corleone.

Specifically, the Fredo we saw in *Godfather, Part II*. He betrayed his family and tipped off Don Corleone's enemies with enough information to set up an (unsuccessful) assassination attempt that would have left him in charge of the Corleone crime family. But Don Michael Corleone figured it all out and while he was *definitely* going to kill Fredo at some point, he couldn't bear for his poor mother to lose another son.

So Fredo lived under guard at the family's Lake Tahoe compound with no real power or authority. He just went out fishing every day for years. Which would seem like a pleasant enough life, but he knew that some day, Momma Corleone would drop dead and the day after the funeral … *blammo.*

That's the existence of my old video machines. Not much to do. Hanging around because I think I still have a bunch of VHS cassettes and old camcorder tapes that I have yet to convert to digital video, as well as a laserdisc or two of movies that have yet to come out on DVD.

But as soon as I no longer have any playable content in those old formats … *blammo.*

(Only I won't have one of my punk underlings do the job *for* me, like Michael Corleone did.)

The common denominator between VHS, LaserDisc, and older non-digital camcorders is the same: analog video and audio connections. Whether they have a fat yellow RCA connector or the higher-grade SVHS plug, your computer has no idea how to deal with that sort of video. Transmogrifying these tapes into something that you can enjoy on your iPhone or iPod Touch will require that you hardware up a little.

THE BASIC IDEA

The conversion process goes like this:

1. Hook the playback machine (the tape deck, the old camcorder, the LaserDisc player) to your computer via a hardware interface.
2. Capture the video to your hard drive.
3. Edit the video and export it to an iTunes-studly format.

This will cost you anything from (a) nothing to (b) hundreds of dollars, depending on what you have lying around the house and how good you'd like the final results to be. The complexity of the process will depend on what software you use.

THE HARDWARE

If you're lucky, you already own a digital camcorder. Unless you got the cheapest model in the store — the one they stock just so the salesman can show off its shortcomings and help sell you the better ones — it has a built-in digital interface that plugs right into your desktop. You can then "play" the video straight into your computer.

Nearly all of these also have an "analog pass through" feature. If you rummage deep down into the box it came in, you'll find a cable with what appears to be a hyperthyroid headphone plug at one end and connectors at the other and that can accept standard analog RCA and SVHS video and audio. If so ... huzzah! You can connect the old analog video player into the camcorder, plug the camcorder into your computer, and use the camcorder as a capture device.

You'll have to operate the old player manually, but the camcorder will perform all the format conversions necessary and the same video editing app you use with digital video from the camcorder will be able to record the incoming signal to your hard drive.

If you *don't* have a camcorder, you'll have to exercise the ancient martial art of Master-Card-Fu. You can buy simple USB-based analog-to-digital interfaces fairly cheap, though.

I really like the hardware made by Pinnacle. Its Dazzle line of hardware is simple, easy to use, and affordable. Check out the range of offerings at www.pinnaclesys.com.

For Windows users, the Dazzle Video Creator Platinum is a solid, all-in-one solution. It'll capture video and also includes simple editing tools that can export video files directly into iTunes, all for $89. Their equivalent Mac offering is the Pinnacle Video Capture ... another all-in-one hardware/software combo, but it'll cost you a full $99 smackers.

Both devices capture high-quality video. If your ambitions aren't that high — or if your source video is somewhat lousy — you might actually want to consider buying a USB TV tuner, like the ones I describe in Chapter 6. Tuners from Hauppage, EyeTV, and others also feature standard analog video inputs and can capture video from VCRs and old camcorders. And they're typically no more expensive than the stand-alone adapters, so in a sense you're buying a video capture device and getting the TV tuner for "free."

But these combination TV tuner-video capture devices typically don't capture analog video as well as the stand-alone devices. With the Pinnacle stand-alone devices, your final video can be nearly as good as the original. There'll be lots of detail and the colors will have a satisfying level of snap. TV tuner hardware is designed to record terrific video from cable TV or an antenna; the analog video inputs tend to be a bit of an afterthought.

The next level up in expense would be something like Canopus's ADVC 110. If you have any experience with technology, you know that when they give a product a name consisting of a random string of numbers and letters, it's going to cost you. Yeah, this device isn't designed for random consumers who want to convert a few home movies and old TV shows. It's for professionals who want the highest level of performance (it captures gorgeous video, from both U.S. and international video formats) and greatest convenience (it doesn't require any special software or drivers; you plug it in and any consumer or professional video editing app that knows how to deal with digital cameras can accept input from the box).

It'll run you about $300. So yeah: The Pinnacle hardware is starting to look better and better, isn't it?

THE SOFTWARE

Onward to editing software. The software you get with the Pinnacle capture hardware (and other gear in its class) tends to be rather basic, like operating a VCR. If you want to do something more ambitious than deleting the commercials from a TV show, you might want to pop for a better app.

If you have a Mac, though, there's really no point in going any farther than the copy of iMovie that came installed on your Mac. It's a simple, powerful, and fully mature editing app, and — because it has an Apple logo on it — you can be sure that when you tell it to export the final video to your iPhone or iPod Touch, the programmers knew what they were doing.

On the PC, there are two good choices. Pinnacle is actually a subsidiary of Avid, the company that makes the professional standard in TV and film editing systems. Its Pinnacle Studio app is dirt cheap at $49 and can export finished video to iTunes for synching.

If you intend to do a *lot* of this sort of thing, you'll probably be happier giving Adobe $99 of your cash for a copy of Adobe Premiere Elements (www.adobe.com). It's filled with time-saving features and attractive little tweaks that let you turn two hours of boring soccer video into six minutes of terrific highlights, toot sweet.

What's the best thing about converting old videos? Well, it comes down to a recurring concern of mine: There's a great deal of fantastic creative work that simply dies because it's never released commercially. Converting the video of your child's first birthday is an obvious win, but let's have a shout-out for all the old TV shows and sporting events that couch potatoes record and which will never be seen again unless someone converts it to digital.

Last Labor Day, I was watching the first couple of hours of the Jerry Lewis Telethon. I was watching some random lower-tier Vegas magician walk through ten minutes of magic-store tricks, followed by Jerry Lewis's son doing his one big hit from that band he fronted in the Sixties.

I was too young to appreciate the heyday of the telethon but I still had to reflect that, in the Seventies, you'd tune into the first couple of hours of this show and you'd see Frank Sinatra singing a duet with Ella Fitzgerald, followed by Sammy Davis, Jr., backed by the Count Basie Orchestra.

Someone has that show on tape. If you do, let me know because I have a Dazzle interface and a desperate need to be entertained.

Glorious Television

The Skim

TV to PC to iPhone ▪ TiVo Series 2 and Windows Media Center ▪
TV to Mac to iPhone ▪ TV to iPhone: the DVD Method

I like the iTunes Store, I *use* the iTunes Store, and I want to *support* the iTunes Store. Those plucky Apple kids are showing a lot of spunk with their little garage startup, and if this is what they want to do after college instead of going on to law school like they've always said they wanted to, well, it breaks their poor mothers' hearts but we always said that we wanted to raise kids with enough confidence and self-reliance to choose their own paths in life. "Just don't get one of those really trashy kind of tattoos," we tell the iTunes Store, hoping that it doesn't make the same mistake we did at that age.

But all too often, folks count on the store as their sole means of acquiring content. It's like fast food: It's quick and it's easy and it's always available. But it's always more money than you need to spend, and it only offers a limited menu.

I'm pretty surprised, for instance, that folks pay $30 to $50 for "season passes" to their favorite shows. If you're willing to be a season behind at all times, that's more than the cost of that same season on DVD … only you don't get the higher video quality or the huge quantity of extras of a DVD.

And if you *don't* want to wait, then, hell, you can buy simple TV tuner hardware that plugs into a USB port, connects directly to your cable or HD antenna, and will record shows and add them to your

TIDBIT

I honestly don't get why *all* the TV tuner cards available for PCs don't directly support iTunes export. I *understand* it — it's a little bit of extra work, plus it's hard to keep up with every new Apple product — but still, I don't get it.

Nonetheless, every PC tuner card I've seen records your TV shows in either MPEG-1 or MPEG-2 format. And both can be converted to an iPhone– or iPod Touch-compatible .mp4 file easily with iTinySoft's $45 Total Video Converter (www.effectmatrix.com). Just locate the recorded file (it might be buried inside the app's Program directory), choose the pre-wired iPod or iPhone configuration, and click.

iTunes library automatically. If you were going to buy two season passes, you've covered the cost of the hardware … and remember, *The Late Show with David Letterman* isn't coming to the iTunes Store anytime soon.

So it's a choice of either the infinite possibilities of cooking your own TV content or spending more money and having a limited range of options. It's a no-brainer.

TV TO PC TO IPHONE

On the Mac, there's really only one choice for TV-recording hardware and software. But on a PC, there's … let's see …

(Ihnatko shoves the edge of his desk and sends self and his chair to the other side of the office; retrieves a big plastic tub full of hardware; crab-walks chair back to the desk.)

… at least nine. But you really only need to know about two of 'em:

Hauppage WinTV

I like Hauppage's gear (www.hauppage.com) because you can select from such a wide variety of consistently high-quality hardware. You can buy a dirt-cheap $55 card that installs inside your desktop PC, a little $80 USB box, a just-as-cheap thing the size of a USB thumb drive that you can easily take with you when you travel, … even big $200 cards that can record digital satellite TV and feature dual tuners so that they can record more than one show at a time.

They all include Hauppage's WinTV tuner/personal-video-recorder software, which is a treat to use. WinTV is available in both conventional analog and bleeding-edge digital TV editions. Unfortunately, the WinTV software doesn't support iTunes directly. But the company offers Wing, a $25 add-on app that can record TV shows directly to your iPhone or iPod Touch by simply clicking a checkbox (see Figure 6-1).

Pinnacle PCTV

Pinnacle's TV tuner line (available in a wide range of USB and PC card flavors; www.pinnaclesys.com) isn't as ambitious as Hauppage's. But it has a clear goal of being as easy to set up and use as a TV set itself. Given that *Clerks: The Animated Series* got cancelled after only two episodes and yet *Family Guy* continues to be a huge hit, you *know* that this translates into a goal to be functional even if the average TV viewer is as dumb as a jar of asphalt.

The other great advantage (from our perspective) is that PCTV is made by a company with a big line of video software

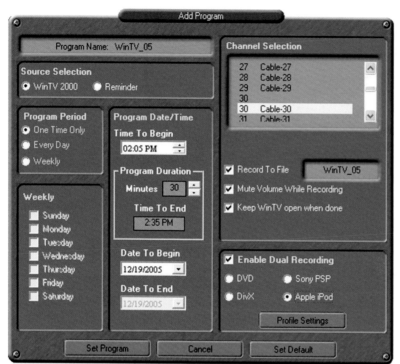

Figure 6-1
Recording WinTV shows to your iPhone on a Wing.

and converters in their catalogue. So PCTV products support the iPhone and iPod Touch right out of the box. Recorded shows can also be easily edited with Pinnacle's companion Pinnacle Studio software; you can easily zap out the commercials and any musical numbers that feature Tony Danza.

Go with Hauppage for overall quality, but go with Pinnacle hardware if you want a functional solution for the least amount of cash.

TIVO SERIES 2 AND WINDOWS MEDIA CENTER

I can tell by the way you're holding this book that you're a person of wealth and taste. It's possible that you already *own* a machine

that records TV shows digitally.

If you have a Windows Media Center PC, or a TiVo Series 2, there's a fab little app that can take its programming, convert them to .mp4 files, and add them to your iTunes library: Roxio's $30 MyTV to Go utility (www.roxio.com).

Figure 6-2 shows the app in action. After a few moments of pointing and clicking, the shows you've recorded will be transcoded into iPhone– and iPod Touch-studly formats and squirted into your iTunes library.

TV TO MAC TO IPHONE

In the grand tradition that's been kept alive by everyone who's ever ignored my

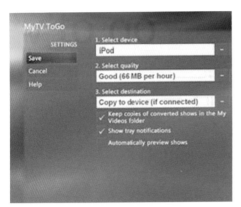

Figure 6-2

Adding iPod support to Windows Media Center Edition with MyTV to Go

Figure 6-3

TV to iPhone PDQ with EyeTV

advice at the start of this chapter and gotten the words "Hot Little Tamale" tattooed across his or her chest on an impulse, I'm going to pretend that something bad is actually exactly the *perfect thing*. Watch me:

"Hey, isn't it terrific that there's pretty much only *one* solution for recording TV on a Mac? Those poor bastards with PCs have to make a decision after looking at almost a *dozen* different options!"

Okay, well, it's not like there's *really* only one piece of tuner hardware and personal-video-recorder software available. For the Mac, there are as many as … um … okay, two.

But the only one I'll tell you about is the EyeTV from Elgato. The hardware and software are head-and-shoulders above anything else. They have a whole line of external boxes that work on nearly all Macs, including conventional and HDTV options.

Check out products and prices at www. elgato.com. As with the Hauppage line, they range from cheap doo-dads that cost $80 to expensive boxes that hope to be the heart of your HD home theater system

As a Mac-only product, the EyeTV soft-

ware is aggressive in its support for iPhones and iPods. Any recorded show can be transcoded to the correct specs and added to your iTunes library with just one click. Yes indeed: It's the big button that looks like an iPod and says, "iPod."

As with almost any transcoding process, it'll take a while before the file's finished (even on an Intel-based Mac, it can take twice the running length of the show). But if you've set EyeTV to record your favorite shows, you can have the app convert the programs for the iPhone or iPod Touch the moment recording is finished. Just choose the iPod option from the Export To pop-up menu, in either the show's schedule detail view, or in the schedule list itself (see Figure 7-4).

Yeah, I know. It should have an option specifically for the iPhone and the iPod Touch. Well, it works fine as it is and once someone at Elgato buys herself an iPhone …

With the iPod export option enabled, by the time you wake up in the morning all the nights' recordings will be waiting for you in your library, ready to be synched to your iPhone or your iPod Touch.

Just don't watch them while you drive. It's very rude to the person you're talking to on the phone in your other hand.

TV TO IPHONE: THE DVD METHOD

I have sort of a genetic attraction toward the "record TV on a computer, have the computer transcode the show to an iPhone-compatible format" solution. When the computer handles everything from start to finish, you feel as secure and at peace as you do when you see the lady at Dunkin' Donuts using tongs *and* wax paper as she boxes your half-dozen.

Figure 6-4

iPod conversion: the zero-click method

But if you're going to go around buying hardware, you probably ought to consider the option of just buying yourself a stand-alone DVD recorder. You can program it to record the output of your cable box just like a VCR, and after you've burned the disc, you can pop it into your PC or Mac and use any DVD-ripper software to convert the shows therein to video files. (Read all about that in Chapter 4.)

And because that DVD isn't copy-protected, you won't even need any of the extra decoding software that the PC apps usually require. It's more complicated than recording shows directly to your hard drive, but maybe you *wanted* to buy a DVD recorder anyway. It's up to you, all right? I'm just trying to be helpful, here.

About 24 hours after I write this, I'll be on a four-hour Amtrak ride from Boston to New York City. So naturally it's very, very important that I check my EyeTV schedules and make sure that it's going to record and transcode about six hours' worth of programming.

Which is in itself a double-edged thing.

I was upfront with you about the nature of this book: If there's even 100K of unused space on your iPhone or iPod Touch, then you just aren't trying hard enough. But, man alive, after you start using your desktop computer as a DVR, your goal stops being "I want to fill this 16-gigabyte device to full capacity" and starts being "Er, you know, I now have less than 20 megabytes of storage on an internal hard drive that had about 200 gigs free before I hooked up the TV tuner box last month."

The sudden lack of free space has made my Mac slow and sluggish. I tell it, "You know what you should do? You should open Photoshop and help me edit these 50 photos I took at the MIT flea market last weekend." The computer takes a few moments to acknowledge me and even then, it clearly would just like to remain inert.

So in the end, a TV tuner box adds an extra level of sophistication to the home-video experience. It's often been said that the purpose of a TiVo or any other personal video recorder is to watch hundreds of hours of TV programming so you wouldn't have to.

With the advent of a little USB peripheral, now your PC or Mac can duplicate the physical effects of so much TV watching as well.

Radio

The Skim

The RadioShark ■ Recording Radio Shows ■
Importing Recorded Audio into iTunes

For many people, an AM/FM radio is an object that only gets pressed into service when (a) there's a baseball or hockey game that's been blacked out from local broadcast or (b) God has sent you a clear and convincing message that he most certainly does *not* count you among his beloved.

Specifically, he's caused you to set off on a three-hour car trip with an iPhone or iPod Touch with only 20 minutes of battery life in it. And you forgot your power adapter.

But don't scoff at radio. It's only at those long, lonely forsaken moments that you come to appreciate the value of radio. Well, yeah, corporate stations I can take or leave (and that first option doesn't count). But local radio is wonderful. We may pride ourselves on being Thoroughly Modern Millies, but there's still something fundamental about interactive community-based call-in shows that a message board will never duplicate.

Besides, radio is a swell source of free content for your iPhone or iPod Touch. It's hard to switch on a $12 radio feeling as though you're Sticking It To The Man. But the fact that you're listening to copyrighted music without paying for it has *got* to have the Recording Industry Association of America upset for *some* bloody reason.

Isn't that enough reason to buy the hardware you need to record radio shows and automatically load them up on your iPhone or iPod Touch?

THE RADIOSHARK

There are a bunch of PC and Mac radio receivers on the market, but I believe that all discussion of what to buy begins and ends with the $49 RadioShark 2 by Griffin Technology (www.griffintech.com). My argument, which I promise you is quite ironclad:

- It's an external USB device, and installs as easily as a mouse.
- It lives up to its marketing tagline as "TiVo for radio." The software makes it dead-simple to schedule regular recordings, and it saves those programs as files that can slurp straight into iTunes without any further ado.
- It's both PC– and Mac-compatible, which means you can move it from system to system, cackling with glee.

And that's all very, very true. But the trump card, the feature that closed down the competition before it ever really started is this:

- It looks like a jet-black shark fin, and it is studded with colored lights (see Figure 7-1).

Figure 7-1
The RadioShark: instant awesome

TIP

It's actually possible to have the best of both worlds these days. Many radio stations are thoroughly modern Millies and they either stream their programming live over the Internet or they go so far as to even package their most popular shows as podcasts. Chapters 13 and 14 teach you what you need to know about finding this online programming and capturing it to your hard drive without buying any actual hardware.

Game, set, and match. There is no piece of office equipment that cannot be immeasurably improved by having a light-up electronic shark fin placed atop it or on a nearby shelf. I mean, come *on*. I've set it atop a 10-year-old box fan here in the office and the box fan is making the iMac look like crap.

RECORDING RADIO SHOWS

To be honest, I might have recommended it even if it didn't actually do anything. Conveniently, the RadioShark works exactly as advertised. Installation takes less than five minutes and leaves you with a radio tuner window on your desktop (see Figure 7-2).

Incidentally, throughout this chapter, I'll be mixing in images from both the Windows and Mac OS versions of the RadioShark software. They're easy to tell apart: The Mac edition looks, well, much shinier.

And the funny thing is, whether you're a Mac or a PC user, you can exploit these differences to underscore your personal prejudices against the other OS. "Typical Mac interface," Windows user sniffs, "Flash over power, style over substance." Mac users are encouraged to admire the fact that a clean and attractive interface is a more *usable* interface.

Of course, the best answer is for these two groups to put their differences aside and unite against their common enemy: their broadband providers. 150K download bandwidth? And they call *that* "high-speed"?!?

Oh, right … the RadioShark. You spin the dial (or just use the Seek button for auto-tuning), you enjoy the sounds as they float through the air, and if you like what you're hearing, you punch the Record button.

Simple, but not simple *enough*: We want to make every episode of Boston's local radio newscast or just next Thursday's Red Sox game as easy to load into our iTunes library as a podcast.

Have no fear: The RadioShark has a full compliment of scheduled-recording features (see Figure 7-3) to handle all that.

You can schedule an event days or even months in advance, and if it's a regular show you can specify that it's a "repeating" show that should be recorded every Sunday, or every weekday, or on whatever schedule you specify. And there's no limit to how many items you can add to the schedule.

As much as I like the RadioShark, I *should* point out that most radio stations are all too aware that you kids today are into flared trousers, Beatles haircuts, and digital music players, and so they offer alternative delivery methods. So before you go the RadioShark route, Google the call letters of

Figure 7-2
The main tuner window (in Windows)

your local stations and see what's available via their Web sites.

Oftentimes, their most popular shows are posted as podcasts shortly after transmission; search through the iTunes Store for those call letters. Or, maybe they simulcast all their programming via streaming audio; in Chapter 13, you can read about software that will allow you to schedule and automatically capture these feeds to audio files. Either way, you might get a cleaner reception through a download than from over the air.

The RadioShark isn't expensive, but it costs more than a copy of *People* magazine, so it's not like it's dirt-cheap. Still, a pal of mine bought one to record one thing and one thing only: the morning traffic report, which is never on precisely when she wants to hear it. No kidding. One five-minute recording that she plays while the car's warming up saves her so much annoyance and time that she says she would have paid double what Griffin was asking for the device.

As for a custom little script that automatically creates a brand-new iTunes playlist of podcasts and music, with the traffic report always inserted into the Number 1 position. *That,* she was more than happy to let me write for free.

Yes, it still stings.

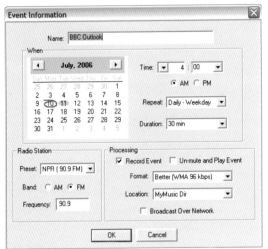

Figure 7-3
Setting up a scheduled recording (in Windows)

Figure 7-4
Putting the morning news onto your iPod automagically — on the Mac, anyhow

IMPORTING RECORDED AUDIO INTO ITUNES

Whether you punch Record manually or allow RadioShark to record shows for you automatically, the app will stash the recording inside your default music folder. That's My Music if you're using Windows, Music if you're on a Mac.

By default, the Windows edition chooses Windows Media as the audio format, with conservative settings that result in tight, compact files. You can downgrade the quality (and get smaller files) by choosing a lower bit rate in the Format pop-up menu when you schedule the recording.

To use these files in iTunes, just drag them into your iTunes library window. iTunes will automatically convert them to the AAC format that iTunes prefers.

On the Mac, RadioShark's app has a little bonus feature: When you click the Add Recordings to iTunes checkbox in the app's Record & Playback preferences, RadioShark

will automatically send the recordings it creates straight into your iTunes library and right into the playlist you specify (see Figure 7-4). By telling iTunes to keep this playlist synched to your iPhone or iPod Touch, your device will always contain the local morning news and traffic when you plug it into your car stereo and begin that brutal, soul-wrenching commute morning after morning.

Until you can't take it any more and just keep right on driving until you reach the Canadian border and your new life as an illegal immigrant. (In which case RadioShark will stop recording new audio once your hard drive back in your old apartment fills to capacity. But that's hardly RadioShark's fault.)

Otherwise, just locate the files inside your Music folder and drag 'em into your iTunes library window.

There are times when I'm convinced that radio is doomed to die a deathly death. But there are also times when I wonder if it's commercial music whose days are numbered. We all have iPhones and iPods and other digital music players and there are a million ways to cause hours and hours of free programming to arrive each and every day and fill up their storage space. Radio is just another source of free content that commercial music has to compete with.

To be honest, iTunes already downloads more podcasts every day than I can possibly listen to. With the addition of the RadioShark, which will grab hours and hours' worth of music and copyrighted sports broadcasts, well, my interest in purchasing the new *American Idol* seasonal ballads CD continues to decline. And it ain't like I was all that interested to begin with.

Comics

The Skim

When I first got my iPhone, I tried using it for just about everything. It's like a chainsaw: It's built for a certain purpose but once you've used it for the task for which it was designed, you spend the rest of the day looking around and thinking, "I wonder if it'll work on *that?*" And the next thing you know, you're at the store shopping for a new sofa.

Not *all* these experiments are that successful, but it turns out that the iPhone and the iPod Touch are fantastic devices for reading digital comic books and online comic strips. It's probably the only handheld that's any good at all at this, actually. It's all thanks to the touch interface. Reading a comic on a small screen involves an endless amount of sliding your tiny viewport around a full-sized printed page. In other devices, that means lots of awkward and imprecise clicking that jumps you a little too far this way or that way. With the iPhone, you just nudge the page a bit with your thumb to tweak the next panel into precise view (see Figure 8-1). It's fab.

COMIC BOOK ARCHIVE FORMATS

The comics industry is still figuring out how to deal with the digital world. There's no iTunes Store for comic books, so DC Comics and Marvel and the rest would have to (shock! horrors!) actually form some kind of partnership that would benefit the industry as a whole, instead of making Captain America fight Batman.

(Did you see that match-up in *JLA/Avengers*? It was awesome.)

So as a result, if you head for official company Web sites, you're likely to see just a handful of promotional comics … and they can be read only online. If you're extremely lucky, you can download them as PDF files, which means you can view them as easily as any other Portable Document Format files. (Check out Chapter 19 for the straight dope; it's about reading all kinds of documents and data on your device. Not just the few data types supported by iTunes.)

But these companies just aren't learning from history. The music industry didn't get on the digital music bus and, as a result, consumers jumped behind the wheel and drove away in it, leaving publishers with no control whatsoever. And the same thing seems to have happened with digital comics.

The community of Internet geeks and the community of comic-book geeks — yes, apparently there's a certain amount of overlap, shockingly enough, including your esteemed correspondent — have come up with a very simple digital comic book format called a Comic Book Archive or Comic Book Reader file. It's become the most popular format for online comics repositories. It's an open format that anybody can support, and there are multiple apps for desktop comic reading available for every OS you can name.

"Okay, I choose the name 'The OS of the iPhone and iPod Touch.'"

Figure 8-1

Oh, Mary Worth, *when* will you learn to shut your piehole and stop meddling?

(Wiseguy.)

Right. Well, no, there isn't a reader for the iPhone or iPod Touch yet. But the good news is that Comic Book Reader files truly are very simple. Each page of the comic is a JPEG image. The individual files are numbered in sequence so they're automatically presented in the correct page order, and they're compressed together into a single file using standard archive formats.

There are two flavors of Comic Book Archive files:

- ◪ Files that end in .cbz are archived in ZIP format.
- ◪ Files that end in .cbr are archived in RAR format.

To load these comics on an iPhone or an iPod Touch, we just need to extract the JPEG images. We can then synch the images to the device's photo library with iTunes, just like any other pictures.

FINDING COMICS ONLINE

Turning a comic into a Comic Book Archive file is no more complicated than ripping a CD or a DVD. In fact, the term "ripping" was actually coined by the process for converting comics to digital files. Your computer's optical drive is the perfect size for optical discs but you can't get a comic book in there unless you physically rip the pages out, fold them once or twice, and jam 'em in there.

Which is a major hassle. But after you've managed to pound the door shut again, the software does all the work.

I'm lying, of course. The only way to "rip" a comic yourself is to scan the pages in manually, one at a time. And you'd probably be sick and tired of even *Sandman #8* by the time you'd finished the job.

So you're really going to have to rely on downloads of CBZ and CBR files. Until the big publishers decide to get into the game, there are only a couple of really big repositories of digital comics. My favorite is http://goldenagecomics.co.uk, which hosts archive files of hundreds of comics that have fallen out of copyright into the public domain.

The *smaller* publishers have gotten behind a commercial site called Pullbox Online (www.pullboxonline.com). It ain't *exactly* an "iTunes Store for Comic Books" but it does have dozens of CBR-format editions of commercial titles, and you can buy 'em for as little as a quarter (see Figure 8-2).

And although there are no shortage of archive files available elsewhere, they're likely to be on the Web sites of individual artists and creators and therefore tough to smoke out with a conventional Google search.

Fortunately, there are plenty of social bookmarking services that can help you out. If someone was traipsing through the Web like Hansel or Gretel and came across a free comic they liked, they might have posted the link to Del.icio.us or Digg. So try these two URLs on for size:

- ❏ http://del.icio.us/tag/cbr
- ❏ http://digg.com/search?section=all&s=cbr+comic

Most digital comics seem to be CBR files, but to search for the other kind just swap

TIP

No, you can't just type "free cbr comics" into Google and get racks and racks of free comics. Way too many hits.

But you *can* use some of Google's power tools to broadly say, "Please search for CBR files located on public Web servers."

Take a deep breath and type this search string into Google's search box:

http://www.google.com/search?hl=en&q=-inurl%3Ahtm+-inurl%3Ahtml+intitle%3A%22index+of%22+%22Last+modified%22+comics+cbr&btnG=Google+Search

Put it all on one line. You'll get back a lonnnng list of links to individual files with no descriptions, but you'll also get some clues to individual sites that

host small collections of comics. (You can replace "comic" with a more specific search term, like "horror," if you like.)

Kudos to www.tech-recipes.com, which is full of little tidbits like this. I was about to build this string myself but hey, cool, they had it all ready to go.

Figure 8-2
Pullbox Online: It ain't the iTunes Store, but y'all can get comics from it.

"cbr" with "cbz" in those search strings. They'll turn up links to both individual books and whole collections.

Mind you, you'll *still* have to wade through plenty of false hits. It certainly doesn't help that there's an excellent (but for our immediate purposes highly annoying) comics news-and-reviews site called Comic

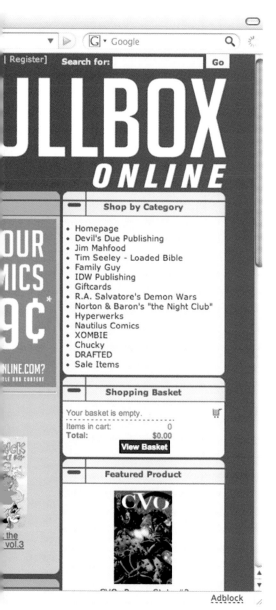

downloaded via BitTorrent without their publishers' consent. When I read a statistic that more than 80 percent of the thousands of comics published since 1962 are available through file-sharing services, it seemed ridiculous. Then I looked. Gorblimey. Any comic you can name is up there, nicely indexed and ready to go.

This is a very itchy situation.

It is clearly — *clearly* — wrong to get comics this way when the books are in print, or available from any bookstore or comic shop as part of a reprint book.

There is absolutely no defense whatsoever for downloading last week's issue of *Birds of Prey* (DC Comics; good stuff) when you can obtain one legally from a nearby store for half the price of a cup of Starbucks coffee.

And *The Watchmen* is a true classic and you really *should* read it, but the collected paperback is by no means hard to find. Decades after publication it continues to be a huge seller. It's never, ever, *ever* going out of print and is available from any mainstream bookstore.

My position softens a bit when it comes to comic books like *West Coast Avengers*. It was published by Marvel back in the Eighties and featured dynamic, meat-and-potatoes-style action and characterization written by Steve Englehart, one of the best writers in the biz.

But that was twenty years ago. It doesn't feature any of Marvel's "superstar" characters and its 100 issues really didn't figure into any major modern Marvel events (well, *House of M*, but I've been trying to pretend that this recent megacrossover event never happened. Marvel seems to be on the same page with me, here). So there's zero chance of it ever being collected and reprinted.

Book Resources (or CBR), but you'll be on your way.

THE UNMENTIONABLES

By far, the *greatest* number of digital comics are copyrighted material illegally being

As a writer myself, I just have this *thing*

about wonderful work that's just allowed to wither and die like that. *WCA* is up there with some of my favorite comics ever, but really, as far as modern audiences are concerned this eight-year-long series might as well have never existed.

The idea of these orphaned books being thrown into the incinerator by their copyright holder isn't a completely accurate comparison, but the image comes readily.

On *this* basis, in the face of Marvel's apparent complete lack of desire for Marvel to gain any revenue from this property, and refusing to overlook the benefits of this material finding some sort of audience, I'm willing to rule that downloading this title from a BitTorrent site doesn't violate the Hippocratic oath ("First, do no harm").

Put a few drinks in me (Oh, bless your heart. Beefeater gin and tonic, not too heavy on the gin, please. And two limes.) and I might even tell you that there's an actual moral imperative to helping this material endure.

In fact, in *my* case I can even unfold a beach chair here on the Moral High Ground. I bought each and every one of those books as individual comics, and I still own 'em all. So Marvel already *has* my money.

I should warn you that BitTorrent is a grotesquely slow, difficult, and unreliable way of getting *anything*. The first time I downloaded a comic collection via BitTorrent, a download that should have taken just an hour or two based on my office's usual speeds took (yes) about a week, as the transmission stopped and started and stopped.

For these and many other reasons I won't explain how to download comics this way. But if you plug a few red-flag words into Google I'm sure you'll find the info.

TRANSMOGRIFYING A COMIC FOR YOUR IPHONE OR IPOD TOUCH

After you've downloaded a CBR or CBZ file, you just have to unpack the individual JPEG images. RAR and ZIP are both hugely popular formats for compressed archive files. There are plenty of utilities that can deal with 'em. Whether you have a PC or a Mac, you can handle the job by downloading just one free utility.

Either way, your first step is to make sure the utility can open the file. They're standard archive files and can be opened with any utility that can deal with RAR or ZIP files, like the commercial WinZip and StuffIt Deluxe apps or some free utilities I'll get to in a sec. But many utilities will take one look at the .cbr and .cbz extension at the end of the filename and leap to the conclusion that it's in some weird alien format.

So, you'll need to end their confusion and change the filename extension yourself. In both Windows Explorer and the Mac Finder, you rename a file by simply clicking its name once to select it, and then clicking it again to edit it. Select the three-letter filename extension. If it was originally .cbr, change it to .rar. If it was .cbz, make it .zip. Now you're ready to unpack the file.

The Windows Side

All you need is a free utility called 7-Zip (www.7-zip.org). You can download it from http://sourceforge.net/projects/sevenzip. It works with both CBR and ZIP files. To unpack files:

1. Use 7-Zip's file browser to navigate to the comic book archive you downloaded.

2. Open it by either double-clicking or pressing Enter or Return. The contents

will appear as a folder (see Figure 8-3).

3. Click the Extract button. A window will pop up that allows you to choose a location for the extracted folder. By default, it points to the same directory as the archive, but you can navigate elsewhere by clicking the ellipsis (…) button.

4. Click OK.

7-Zip will spit out a folder of JPEG files, which you can then synch to your iPhone's or iPod Touch's photo library just as you would any other pile of pictures. Because the files are numbered sequentially, they'll stay in their proper order so long as you don't manually slide them around in a photo album or something like that. (Turn to Chapter 20 for complete instructions on synching photos to your iPhone or iPod Touch.)

The Macintosh Side

The Mac Finder has a built-in extractor for ZIP files. To unpack the archive, just double-click the file. It'll soon be joined by a folder bearing the same name as the archive.

For RAR files, head on over to www.stuffit.com/mac and download a free copy of StuffIt Expander. Expander is what's known as a "helper" application. It doesn't really have a user interface of its own. Like extracting a ZIP file, when you double-click the file, Expander discreetly

Figure 8-3
Extracting comics with 7-Zip

launches, unpacks the archive into a folder next to the original archive file, and then disappears again.

To get it going, you just need to tell the Finder that it ought to hand off all RAR files to Expander from now on. You do this via the file's contextual menu:

1. Right-click the RAR file (or Control+

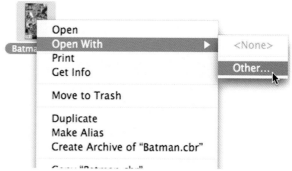

Figure 8-4
Teaching the Finder to unpack RARs with StuffIt Expander

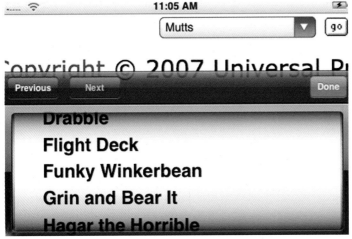

Figure 8-5
Scrolling through the funny pages on the *Seattle P-I*'s site

sorted in their proper page order, which you can now synch to your iPhone or iPod Touch in the simple and glorious manner so eloquently demarcated in yonder Chapter 20.

STRIPPING FOR FUN

This *is* a chapter about comics, so I ought to also talk about using your iPhone or iPod Touch to read comic strips online. There really isn't much of a trick to it. There's no special app or resource. It's no more complicated than knowing about a few newspapers with *wonderful* Web sites that put dozens of strips up on one convenient page:

□ *The Seattle Post-Intelligencer* (www. seattlepi.com). Tops for iPhone and iPod Touch users. Not only do they have dozens of the best strips (*Dilbert, Mutts, Pearls Before Swine*) but every individual strip contains a pop-up menu that lists all the *rest* of the strips. So yes, you *do* have to peer closely at the screen to tap on your first selection, but from then on, it's like you're using an app that was designed for maximum convenience (see Figure 8-5).

□ *The Houston Chronicle* (www.chron. com). It's not quite as convenient as the *Seattle P-I*, but they have two huge columns of comics to choose from. Any strips that are missing from the other site are probably right here.

click it if you only have one mouse button). A contextual menu should pop up (see Figure 8-4).

2. Choose Open With ▶ Other. Normally, the Finder would populate that list with apps that know what to do with this kind of file. Alas, it has no clue, so it's up to you. A standard file browser appears.

3. Navigate to the Applications folder (or wherever you installed the app) and select StuffIt Expander.

Now you can unpack this archive (and all others like it) simply by double-clicking it.

I ought to point out that with this particular kind of file, it isn't even necessary to change the file type to RAR. If you leave the name as is and associate it with Expander, the Finder will simply hand the file off to Expander without any further ado.

Ditto for CBZ files, though in this case you need to associate that type with Expander as well.

You now have a folder of JPEG files,

Yahoo News (http://news.yahoo.com/comics). I'll include this one just for the sake of completeness. Every online comics page subscribes to a different collection of strips and if this is the only place where you can find all your six must-read strips together on one page, well, there y'go. One neat thing about Yahoo: The other sites don't post the day's strip until midnight local time. Yahoo posts them at midnight *Eastern* time. So it's a chance to get an advance peek at *Doonesbury* and maybe win a couple of bar bets.

And I can't resist throwing a little love in the direction of some of my favorite online-only comic strips. Most of these are true kitchen-table productions, written, drawn, and published by a single creator. Some of 'em have been doing this for close to a decade and have carefully built such a following that they now make their living from their creations … and as the saying goes, when you own the company, you're always the first one to get paid.

- *Player vs. Player* (www.pvponline.com). Scott Kurtz has a wonderfully lively drawing style that makes me think he would have made a hell of an animator. Nine years' worth of strips mean you can start with *PVP* the day you reached this page in the book and spend a week reading 'em all. There's a pretty good chance that you'll want to.
- *Dork Tower* (www.dorktower.com). Like *PVP*, *Dork Tower* lets you visit the world of hard-core gamers (of all kinds, from role players to LARPers to card gamers to PSP jockeys and every flavor unnamed).
- *Girls with Slingshots* (www.girlswithslingshots.com). I love Dan-

ielle Corsetto's drawing style, I love her perspective, and I love the fact that she's built a creative world in which a cast of fully realized male and female characters and a talking cactus can both exist in the same space. That's no mean feat.
- *Diesel Sweeties* (www.dieselsweeties.com) actually made the big time. It was published online for a while but was eventually picked up by a syndicate. Richard Stevens still creates online-exclusive strips, which he posts alongside archives of the print strip.

I'm plugging these for no other reason except that I like 'em and read every one of 'em regularly. Also, they've been around long enough that I'm serenely confident that they'll still be around in two years.

COMICS AREN'T JUST FOR KIDS. REALLY!

When you first picked up this book and looked at my photo on the back, you probably thought "Good God, now *here's* the sort of grown man who still reads comic books."

You know, prejudice, bigotry, and snap judgments are ugly, useless things. They jam a potato in the collective tailpipe of the engines of the progress of society.

(And there's nothing wrong with reading comic books in your thirties. *Nothing wrong.* Shut up!!!)

Well, gee, who's the bigger loser? The loser, or the loser who just spent half an hour *reading* about what the loser does? Huh?

Let's just put this whole incident behind us and move on. Friends?

Okay, well, friends or not, I *still* have your money. So there.

PART III

The Internet

News, Blogs, and Bookmarks

The Skim

Digg ⬛ Newsvine ⬛ Blogs and Newsreaders ⬛
Bookmarks ⬛ Finding Online Gems with Del.icio.us

I have many, many different computers here in the office. Naturally, they all have browsers (most have more than one of 'em installed) and the funny thing is that the single feature I use the least is the tool for creating and managing bookmarks.

If the bookmarks feature were an actual book, it would be that copy of *Ulysses* I have on my shelf. It would have a pristine spine and make little crackling noise as I open it.

Nonetheless, I stay on top of about two dozen really important sites and services on a daily basis and probably — no, let me check — *exactly* 741 minor ones. I really couldn't work with so many URLs if I relied on a browser's bookmarks file. Instead, I rely on a host of Web-based services that manage my bookmarks, pre-read all of my favorite sites *for* me so I can tell at a glance if there's anything worth reading, and help me find wunnerful new sites and bits of information on a daily basis.

(Thus compounding the problem by adding more sites to the watch list.)

So it's very *nice* that iTunes automatically keeps my desktop browser bookmarks and my iPhone and iPod Touch in synch. I'm grateful. But take my advice and go bigger.

"You have reached the end of the Internet. Please turn around."

Yes, dear readers, there was a time when such a Web page really existed. Not really, but you know what I mean.

The first time I got a Web browser working was during the George Bush, Sr., administration, and it hooked me so hard that within the space of a week I had methodically clicked through every path I could find, using the same basic obsessive-compulsive (and, frankly, dateless) mindset I'd use if I were exploring a series of caves in an adventure game. Eventually, I imagined that I'd actually seen every page that existed on the Web. If I didn't, I'm sure I came pretty dang close.

Today, that's just not impossible. If you tried to replicate it, pretty soon you'd hit one of those Web pages that causes you to furiously click Ctrl+Z or ⌘+Z on your brain so that you could somehow un-see that image.

DIGG

No, you can't sling your Quiver of Ever True +5 Paladin Arrows and go out exploring the Internet. You have to allow the cool and interesting sites to come to *you*. Which is why you need to bookmark www.digg.com/iphone on your iPhone or iPod Touch.

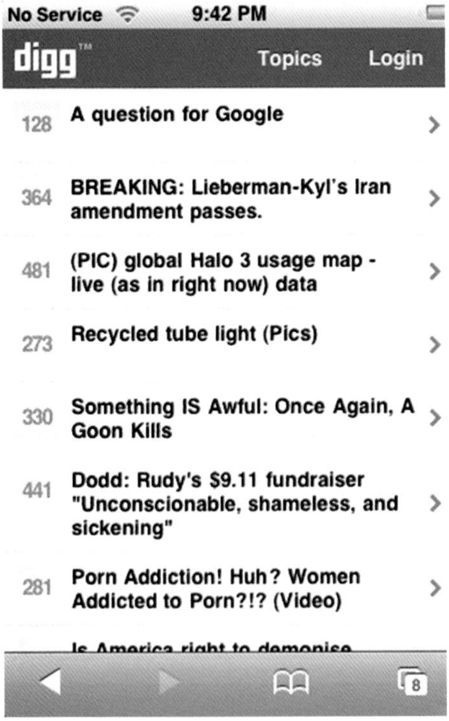

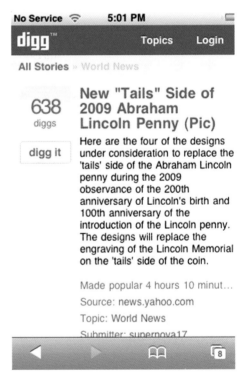

Figure 9-1
Digg shows you the freshest Web pages and stories posted by its huge international community of users.

Figure 9-2
Digg lets you try before you buy.

Figure 9-1 shows you Digg's initial welcome page. A moment of silence, please, for a truly wonderful online iPhone app. It's a real treat to work with.

It's really a powerful concept. Digg is free for everybody. If in your usual online travels you happen to come across a Web page that you like, you can submit it to Digg. Ultimately, if *lots* of people are recommending this page and the frequency with which it's been recommended is accelerating, algorithms at Digg flag it as an item of particular interest and it lands on Digg's directory of new and wonderful links, which is updated nearly in real time.

Figure 9-1 shows you the top page of general-interest items. But if you just want to know what's going on in the world of sports, world news, entertainment, the environment, or just about anything, you can tap the Topics button and select a category from a list of about four dozen subcategories.

If one of these headlines leaps out at you, give it a tap and you'll be taken to a page that describes the content (see Figure 9-2). Wow, 638 people seem to think that this story about the new Lincoln penny is the bee's knees in the cat's pajamas. I'll tap on the headline to go to the actual Web page and read the article.

I like Digg because it casts a wide net. The top page will link to a PDF file of a David Hasselhoff paper doll. But the next item in the listing will be a *Wall Street Journal* story about furious lobbying to overturn a key piece of legislation that keeps the whole mortgage industry afloat. Then it's a YouTube of some kid trying to play "Radar Love" on a cheap guitar using only his feet, then a revealing interview with a presidential candidate's chief of staff, …

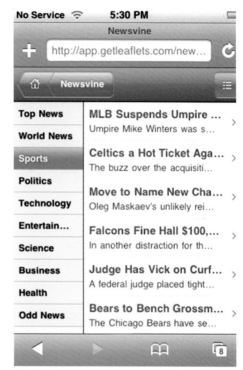

Figure 9-3
Newsvine clips the top news from some of the most trusted sources.

Digg is the perfect answer to the question "What are people interested in and talking about right now?" Editors of metro newspapers look at all of the stories that are coming in and make a judgment about what's interesting and important enough to publish. Digg makes the same decisions, based on voting and lots of math.

NEWSVINE

Newsvine (www.newsvine.com) is my other main iPhone online app for news. It's based on the same basic premise as Digg — users "vote" on news stories that they think more people should read — but it's a bit more straightlaced than Digg. There's a greater tendency to find stories that link to major news outlets rather than some dude's MySpace blog.

Also like Digg, it's a general browser-oriented service except that someone's gone to the trouble of building a nice iPhone interface. You'll find this app inside the jack-of-all-trades app Leaflets (www.getleaflets.com). Tap the Newsvines button and you'll see everything nicely organized for you as in Figure 9-3.

I wish the screen weren't quite so cluttered, but at least when you tap a headline, the app opens the actual story and formats it for the iPhone's or iPod Touch's screen.

BLOGS AND NEWSREADERS

Everyone brings their own specific needs to a smartphone. Some want killer e-mail, others want to manage blazing furies of incoming and outgoing calls, while others really want a great media player that can also be used to call out for pizza.

I've had smartphones for several years now and, to me, the killer feature of an Internet-enabled phone is its ability to access newsreader and blog aggregator services like

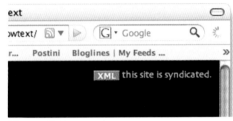

Figure 9-4
The RSS icon in the address line tells you the site has, well, an RSS feed. You may also see other indicators on the Web pages themselves, like the XML button.

Bloglines (www.bloglines.com) and Google Reader (www.google.com/reader). They're free online services that act practically like a TiVo for the Web. You tell it what sites and blogs you're interested in, and it'll keep an eye on 'em for you. And when you're in the mood for a little readin', they'll direct you to all the pieces on that site that are new and interesting.

The next time you wander through the Web using Internet Explorer or Firefox or the desktop edition of Safari, keep an eye peeled on the right side of the browser window's address bar. On most sites, you'll see a little icon like the one in Figure 9-4. In Safari, it's a little blue pill marked RSS.

On the Web page itself, you might also see something like that orange XML badge and the proud legend "This Site Is Syndicated."

These are great things to see. And it's not that sort of mixed-blessing reaction you have when you peek into the kitchen of your favorite restaurant and spot three full rat traps. "Maybe this means they got 'em all," you think, hopefully, because you've already eaten too much of your Oddly Crunchy Chicken Pie to have much of a chance of

TIDBIT

For more info about RSS and the awesome things your iPhone or iPod Touch can do with it, check out Chapter 10, which is a series of tricks and techniques for exploiting RSS. Many of my most favoritest shortcuts for the iPhone are in that chapter.

refusing to pay the check.

No, a Web site with syndicated content is incontrovertible good news for you, the home viewer. Those syndication badges mean that the Web site contains a little catalogue file that documents and summarizes all its content. That file (known as a "syndication feed") is updated every time new material is published on the site.

But it isn't designed to be read by humans. It's there to be loaded and examined by software that can analyze that data to decide what's new and interesting on the site. It can even determine which articles you've already read and what's been posted since your last visit.

Figure 9-5

The desktop version of Bloglines: millions of words of Web content distilled into one page

Let Bloglines and Google Reader Do the Work for You

The upshot is that instead of hitting hundreds of sites just to see if they've been updated recently, and *then* hoping that some of the content is actually interesting, these online apps do that work *for* you.

Take a look at my current desktop Bloglines view (see Figure 9-5). It ain't the iPhone edition, but it'll explain the basic concept. The column on the left contains some of the hundreds of blogs and news sites that I've told Bloglines to watch. The fact that they're showing up in the list at all means that there are articles that I haven't read yet; the number to the right of the name tells me how many.

I've clicked AppleInsider (a great news site for information on upcoming Apple releases) and presto, Bloglines shows me a tidy little list of article summaries. If I want to read more, I can just click the headline and go to the actual Web page.

Many Web sites don't just syndicate summaries of articles. This little catalogue file contains the entire article itself, which I can then read without leaving Bloglines.

Bloglines has a very slick iPhone edition of its service that can be accessed at http://i.bloglines.com (see Figure 9-6). As if the desktop edition weren't good enough! With this version, I can eat a quick sandwich with my right hand and keep up with all my news sites with the other.

Figure 9-6
Bloglines: the iPhone experience

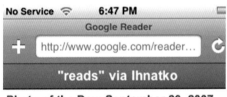

Figure 9-7
Google Reader, à la iPhone

I created Figure 9-6 on my iPhone just a minute or so after clicking on AppleInsider on my desktop in Figure 9-5. Notice something interesting?

Yup: In the later screenshot, AppleInsider no longer appears in the list of unread blogs. Because, y'know, I've just *read* it. That's another big advantage of using Bloglines or Google Reader to manage your blogs and

news. I can bring up that window on my Mac, on my PC, on my iPhone, on a pal's iMac while I'm away visiting him for the weekend, … and because all my bookmarks are being managed by that same service, *all* my bookmarks are *always* available to me, no matter what browser I use when I log into Bloglines. And it *always* knows which articles I've read and which ones are still fresh.

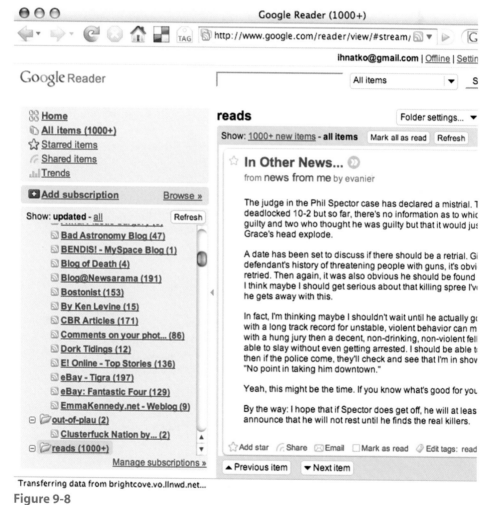

Figure 9-8
Google Reader, the desktop edition

Figures 9-7 and 9-8 show you the iPhone and desktop editions of Google Reader, respectively. Plug www.google.com/reader/m into your iPhone or iPod Touch to use the mobile edition. The desktop edition is at www.google.com/reader.

I think both Bloglines and Google Reader are equally fab newsreaders. I believe Google Reader is easier to use with smaller collections of blogs and sites, while Bloglines makes it easy for me to get a quick and clear overview of what's happening on hundreds of Web sites at once.

Both services allow you to build collections of subscriptions. One for news, one for your friends' blogs, one for online comic strips, … each one cutting your enormous toilet-paper-like scroll of subscriptions down to just the handful you want to focus on at any given moment.

The real difference between the two is in how you use 'em. I like how Bloglines makes it easy to point-and-shoot on the blogs that seem to scream out to you. Google Reader's default behavior is to put allllll the new items from allllll your blogs together on one roll. Which is swell if you're just managing a handful of subscriptions, or if you take the time to tag and organize them all.

Otherwise, it's a bit of a hassle to slog through four pages of unread entertainment gossip before you get to that critical local news item. If you'd been using Bloglines, your eyes would have been drawn to "Boston Traffic Watch" right away and before you left the office for the day you would have known that three tractor-trailer loads of bacon, eggs, and toast overturned on I-95 this afternoon. As it is, you won't be seeing your spouse and kids before it's time to peel breakfast from the treads of your tires and send them off to

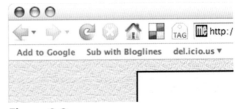

Figure 9-9
You add bookmarks to these services from any browser window, via "bookmarklets" that you install yourself.

school in the morning.

Bottom line: Sign up for free accounts on both and then a month or two later, figure out which one has collected more of your bookmarks. *That* one has earned your loyalty.

Adding Subscriptions to Bloglines and Google Reader

After you've found a syndicated Web site that you want to keep track of, you can save the URL in Bloglines or Reader by pasting its URL into a special "subscribe" form found on the service's Web site. The service can fill in all of the details just by looking at the site's syndication feed.

But both services offer a much quicker and simpler mechanism: a Subscribe to This Web page "bookmarklet" that you add to your browser's bookmarks bar. With one of these bookmarklets installed, you just click the bookmarklet and a subscription to whatever blog or news site you happen to be eyeing at the moment will automatically be added. Figure 9-9 shows you my normal browser window, kitted out with bookmarks for both sites (plus a third that I'll mention soon).

You can find Bloglines's bookmarklet at www.bloglines.com/help/easysub. Google sure doesn't make its bookmarklet easy to find,

> **TIP**
>
> Bloglines and Google Reader have an extra little feature: They allow you to search blog postings for a specific term or phrase.
>
> That's damned handy, particularly when you're trying to find opinions of the general public or trying to get a bead on a story that's so new that the major news organizations have yet to really pick up on it.
>
> I'm not ashamed to admit it — I mean, I'm ashamed that I *do* this, but I'm not particularly ashamed to cop to it to you nice folks — but after I give a talk to a large audience or make an appearance on network TV … well, yeah, I do a blog search to see what people have to say about it.
>
> It's not so much an ego thing so much as it's a way to figure out if people were creeped out by the way I was staring at that duck that I spotted just outside of camera range.

but if you go to the official Google Reader blog (http://googlereader.blogspot.com) and use the built-in Search box to look for "little Google buttons," you ought to find it.

Both Bloglines's and Google Reader's bookmarklets install the same way, no matter which desktop browser you use. Just drag it *straight* off the Web page and into your browser's Bookmarks bar, below the address bar.

BOOKMARKS

First, we talked about Digg and Newsvine. One of their big features is that everything that lands on those services has been "certified" as a good article by virtue of the fact that dozens of people independently chose to post it to the service.

Then we moved on to Bloglines and Google Reader. Amongst their ginchiness: They allow you to collect all your important bookmarks in one central location, so that (a) you can enjoy them from any of your many Internet-studly machines, and (b) you can add to your iPhone or iPod Touch browser experience without having to be physically behind the computer that synchs data to the device.

Del.icio.us (yup, that's the actual URL: del.icio.us) combines the two (see Figure 9-10). It's a free service that allows you to post bookmarks for any site you want to remember, and you can post to it the same way you post to Bloglines or Google Reader.

A bookmarklet in your browser's address bar grabs the URL and adds it to your collection. Click the Help link at the top of the main Del.icio.us page to add this magical bookmarklet to your browser.

Or, you can add links by copy and pasting them into a new entry manually, via Del.icio.us's Web page.

It even allows you to tag the page with descriptive keywords, so you can easily find it later. The column on the right shows some of the hundreds of tags I've added in the past couple of years. Clicking on iPhone immediately takes me to all of the neat iPhone resources I've found since the product was first announced.

It's a huge transformation of how you use

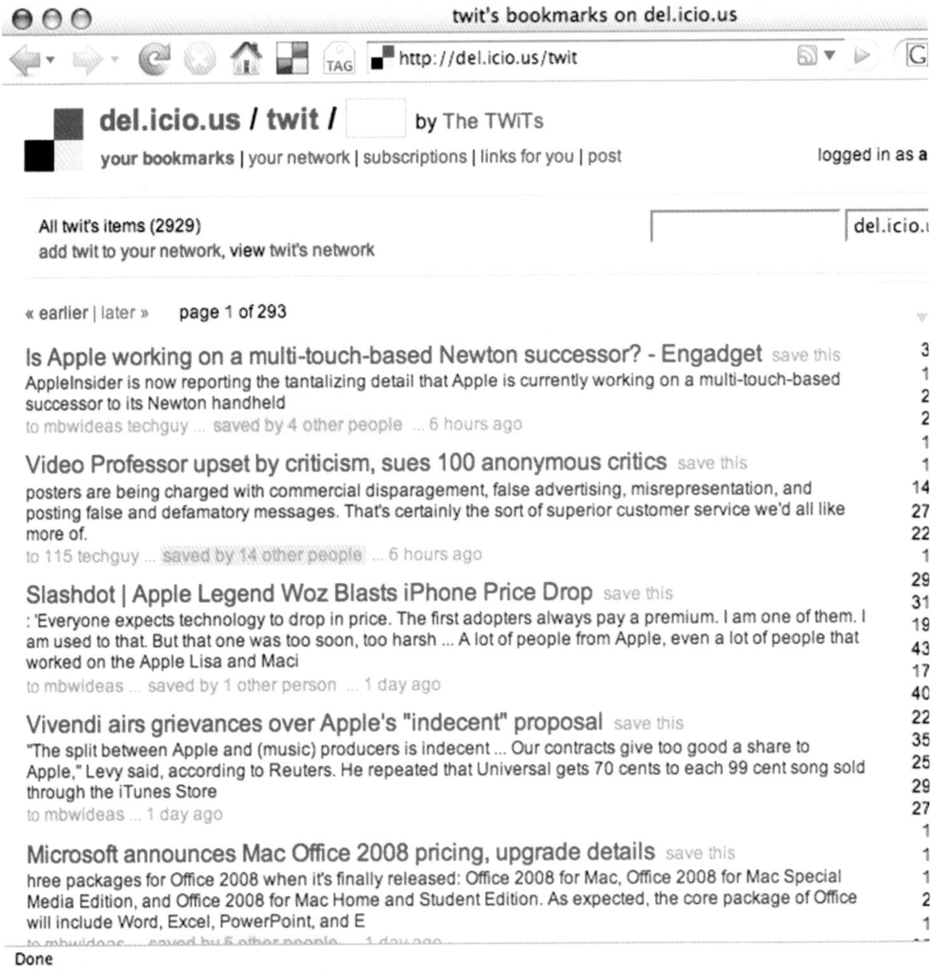

Figure 9-10
Del.icio.us holds all your bookmarks in one central location.

the Web. How often have you wracked your brains thinking, "Now, *what* was that awesome blog I happened across the other night? The one about that former sound engineer for the Letterman show who now restores Ferraris full-time?"

Normally, you'd be stuck. But once you accept Del.icio.us into your life, you can go to the service's page, log in to your account

if you haven't already, and simply search your bookmarks for anything tagged with "Ferrari." And there they are, listed in the order in which you posted them.

Compare and contrast this with the experience of bookmarking sites locally. You have a Mac at home, a PC at the office, and a third computer in the family room, as well as a BlackBerry that your boss makes you carry

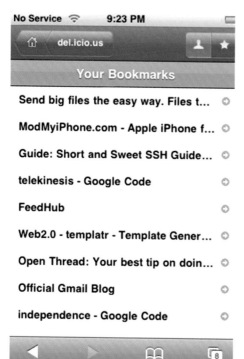

Figure 9-11

Your saved del.icio.us bookmarks, presented via Leaflets

around on business trips. Which browser's bookmarks file contains the link?

Accessing your Del.icio.us bookmarks on your iPhone isn't *quite* as convenient as using bookmarks that you've synched via iTunes. But it's no more complicated than merely storing a bookmark for (once again) the wonderful and ambi-useful Leaflets app (that URL again: www.getleaflets.com). It has a button for accessing your Del.icio.us bookmarks (see Figure 9-11).

Even the regular Del.icio.us Web page looks just fine in Safari and allows you to access some of Del.icio.us's bigger features, like being able to search your bookmarks for specific tags and descriptions.

And there's more …

FINDING ONLINE GEMS WITH DEL.ICIO.US

When you search for something via Google, all you get back are Web pages that match the terms you specified. There's *supposed* to be some sort of ranking system, but it's concealed in swirly purple mists of both mumbo and jumbo and you have to kiss a great many frogs before you find the one link that made the whole undertaking worthwhile.

But let's revisit one important detail of how bookmarks arrive on Del.icio.us: *Someone thought this bookmark was so valuable that he didn't want to forget it.*

That's a pretty solid endorsement, wouldn't you say?

That's why when I'm hoping to find something *specific* on the Web, my first weapon isn't Google. It's Del.icio.us. If I'm looking for a good, free antispyware utility, a Google search will turn up dozens if not hundreds of online ads from companies trying to sell me something. But if I plug "antispyware," "utility," and "free" into Del.icio.us's search box, the gems are immediately apparent. Sure, there will be some duds, but hey, will ya look at that: There's a link that's been saved by more than 3,200 users. I'm guessing that this is a terrific resource.

Similarly, you should make use of Del.icio.us's Popular and Recent links, for a look at what the world seems to be interested in all of a sudden. For your convenience, you can even bookmark direct links to those lists: del.icio.us/popular and del.icio.us/recent.

It really is marvelous, the way they've organized this service. You can bookmark searches for *any* tag in plain English. If you're interested in the Red Sox, for example, bookmark del.icio.us/tag/redsox. It'll always take you to del.icio.us's newest Red Sox-related tags. You can perform searches on more than one word ("redsox" and "Yankees") by separating them with plus (+) signs.

I'm sitting back in my chair now and trying to figure out if I've done a good thing or not.

Bookmarks are dead-simple. They're effective, they're handy, and they do the job they were designed to do. Couldn't be easier to use, either.

But somehow … *that's just not enough.*

Some of us — yes, mainly I'm thinking "me" — have to pervert this Zenlike perfection by introducing new twists that add new power and functionality. That's fine, but now I have you people trying to tap out bizarre nonsensical URLs like del.icio.us.

Well, if I'm too weak to resist the urge to muck things up, at least I'm following in some fairly illustrious footsteps. God created the egg. Smooth, round, meditatively beautiful. He *could* have left well enough alone, but what did he go and do?

He had a platypus break out of it. Go figure.

10

What a Friend We Have in RSS

The Skim

Funny, isn't it, that none of the commercials for the iPhone or the iPod Touch mention that the built-in Safari Web browser features a fairly mature, self-contained RSS/XML reader. Because as far as I'm concerned, the features on this iPhone thing are ranked thusly:

1. Desktop-class Web browser and e-mail.
2. Best pocket media player anywhere.
3. Awesome RSS support in the Web browser.
4. Something about being able to place and receive phone calls or something. I don't know, I wasn't really listening too hard to the announcements.

I mean, we were all pretty keen to get our hands on the iPhone after it was first announced, but there are so many features you don't really appreciate until you start walking around with the thing in your pocket. I couldn't have predicted that Safari RSS would have made it into that list of the most useful features about the iPhone, and yet here I am, sneaking in a whole chapter about it.

It's great to use this feature for the purpose for which it was intended (skim through summarized views of certain RSS-enabled Web sites and blogs), but there are so many ways to *exploit* this that I couldn't resist sharing a few of 'em here.

ABOUT RSS

RSS stands for "Really Simple Syndication." Colloquially, it refers to the "newsfeed" of a Web site. There's the site itself, with all of the words and pictures laid out nicely in pages for the benefit of the humans, but then there's a little file tucked away on the server that contains all that information in a nice, structured database-y sort of format.

Software can examine the feed and have a more intimate relationship with the site's content. When you provide a Web browser with the site's URL, it has to download all of the photos and graphical doodads and ads and columns of links and stuff. When the RSS feed is opened by a piece of software (like Safari's Reader feature), it can sift through all of that data and then just display headlines and summaries of stories that are new since the last time you visited the place.

It actually delivers two kinds of flexibility because it pretty much hands off the site's raw data to the software of your choice. This software can search, sort, and filter the data in any way you choose, and it has complete control over how that data is formatted and displayed, too. A Web page is concrete; a Web site's feed is clay.

Chapter 9 talks about two great news *aggregators* — apps that mashes feeds from several sites together and molds it to your whim — that I like a lot. And both aggregators let you exploit all their features through a lovely Web-based iPhone app.

But Safari has its own built-in RSS reader. If you visit my blog at www.cwob.com, you'll

Figure 10-1
Yellowtext, my humble blog

see it as a regular Web page (see Figure 10-1). But if you zoooooooom in on the upper-corner of the blog, you'll notice a funny-looking

Figure 10-2
When you see one of these symbols on a Web page, it's usually a link to the site's RSS feed.

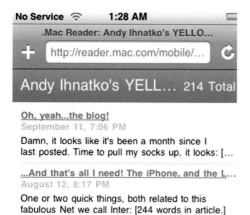

Figure 10-3

My blog, re-interpreted by Safari as just a pile of streamlined iPhone-screen-filling content

orange XML logo (see Figure 10-2). That's one of the universal symbols meaning "this button is a link to the site's RSS feed." If you tap the button, Safari will read and process the feed, and then you'll see my blog presented as in Figure 10-3. Safari opens only the actual Web site when I tap the headline of an article I want to read, and then it'll open the page with the viewer aimed on that specific article.

If you tap the New Bookmark button while you're looking at the RSS view, Safari will generate a bookmark to this RSS feed and not to the Web page itself. So every time

you open this bookmark, you'll open the site in its RSS view.

Gosh, Figure 10-3 makes my blog look purty. This brings us nicely to the Number 1 reason I use Safari's RSS reader.

GETTING A FASTER, CLEANER VIEW OF YOUR FAVORITE SITES

If I'm about to bookmark a page that I'm apt to visit often, I'll hunt for the page's RSS feed instead of bookmarking the page directly. Because it's *always* faster and more convenient to see all a site's content in one slick, scrolling list of plain text than as a Web page.

Particularly when you don't have a high-speed Wi-Fi connection to the Internet from your iPhone or iPod Touch. When you access a site's RSS feed, your iPhone only has to download a small amount of text. When you access the page itself, Safari has to download every article, every photo, every ad, every *everything*.

But RSS isn't just a way of reading Web pages. Syndication is such a powerful, flexible, and ubiquitous concept on the Web that it tends to turn up in the strangest places.

BOOKMARK USEFUL WEB SEARCHES AS RSS FEEDS

No kiddin'. Many sites not only let you do searches, but the server will deliver the results of that search as an RSS feed that it will build on-the-fly for you. Some examples:

- **eBay**. Do a search and then examine the results closely. Aha! Look at the bottom of the search results: There's that familiar orange syndication logo. Give it a tap, and you'll see what Figure 10-4 shows — assuming you were searching

Figure 10-4
An eBay search, bookmarked as a nice, efficient RSS feed

Figure 10-5
RSS search results shows you all the info you'd get if you were actually looking at eBay's Web page.

for *Star Wars* memorabilia, of course. And if you tap an individual auction item, you'll note that eBay's search feed actually returns a very rich experience. You can see pretty much everything you'd see if you were looking at the actual Web page (see Figure 10-5).

▸ **Technorati blog search**. Yes, I know. You *never* search for your own name to see if people are talking about you. Never, ever, ever. But conceptually, if you *were* ever that full of yourself, you could bookmark it (www.technorati. com) and any time the whim struck, you could see what those lying jerks are doing while your back is turned.

▸ **Digg user-recommended Web sites**. As I show in Chapter 9, Digg (www. digg.com) has a nice iPhone-specific Web app for browsing what's hot on the Web — sites that have been recommended and posted to the service by the community of Digg users. But you don't need to use it, really, because each section and search is backed by RSS and, if you're specifically interested in news and sites about beekeeping, you can bookmark an RSS feed that always contains the most recently recommended sites about apiaries and smokers and, um, other things that beekeepers are interested in.

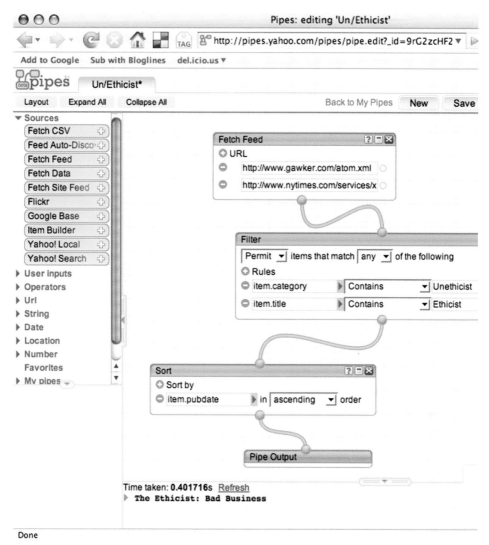

Figure 10-6
Yahoo Pipes lets you build RSS feeds that don't already exist, but should.

Indeed, nearly every service you can name is wired with RSS. Open del.icio.us/tag/iphone+apps to see the latest hot iPhone apps that have been posted to the Del.icio.us service. Then click the RSS badge on the page and bookmark it. Presto: You'll never be more than a step away from finding something ginchy to run on your iPhone.

I swear, your eyes will become so keenly tuned for spotting RSS badges on Web pages as a hawk's are for spotting small, scared, scampering things in a meadow.

SHMUSHING SEVERAL RSS FEEDS INTO ONE

Sometimes no one RSS feed can collect the info you want. Take online comic strips, for example. They're usually published online by their creators. These strips are wonderful but do I really want to click forty separate links each and every morning while I eat my Froot Loops?

Fortunately, there are some simple tools that allow you to build your *own* RSS feeds. My favorite tool is hosted by Yahoo and it's called Yahoo Pipes (http://pipes.yahoo.com).

On your desktop browser, you literally sketch out what you'd like your new RSS feed to look like. It's really very simple. Figure 10-6 shows you one of my pipes. "The Ethicist" is a great column on the *New York Times* site that answers questions about ethics sent in by readers. Gawker publishes a funny parody of the column called the "*Un-Ethicist*" (www.gawker.com/news/unethicist) that answers the same questions, but from a slightly different point of view.

I like both columns and this pipe mashes them together into a single feed.

It's actually doing two tricky things. Neither "The Ethicist" nor its parody have their own dedicated RSS feeds. They just occasionally appear as part of a larger firehose of content from the *New York Times* and Gawker. But this pipe searches the RSS feeds from www.nytimes.com and www.gawker.com, culls only those articles that match those two column titles, and then combines them into a single new feed that I can subscribe to in Safari.

There are tons of ways to exploit this. One of my other fave pipes is that "Morning Funnies" RSS feed, which puts all of my favorite morning Web comics into one lonnnng roll

Figure 10-7

Tracking down the podcast's RSS feed

like the comics section of a paper. Two dozen individual links have been combined into one single bookmark.

Oh, and I certainly can't let you go before telling you …

ONE OF THE BEST TIPS IN THIS WHOLE DAMNED BOOK

… because — wouldn't you know it? — it takes advantage of Safari's RSS reader.

I love my iPhone, my iPod Touch, and all my iPods. But there's one feature present in nearly every other media player — even the cheap ones that you buy at the drugstore — that I sorely covet: the ability to spontaneously put new music or video on the device without having to run your desktop media manager.

With SanDisk's Sansa player, for instance, if I've just ripped a new DVD on my smokin' fast desktop PC, I can just plug the player into the desktop. It'll appear to that PC as a storage device. I simply copy the new video file onto the device and I'm good to go.

But if I want to put that file on my iPhone, I have to copy it onto a flash drive or something, then import it into the one iTunes library that synchs to my iPhone. Never mind that it takes up a whole gigabyte

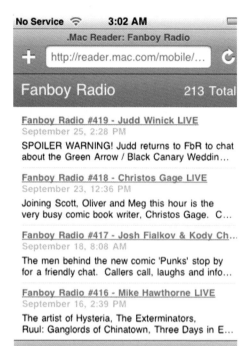

Figure 10-8
Your podcast, shown as a list of RSS show descriptions

Figure 10-9
A link to the actual online MP3 file is embedded in the episode description.

of precious disk space and I have absolutely no desire to ever play it on my desktop. Then I have to do a whole synch.

iTunes has to act as the concierge to *every*

piece of media you want to play via your iPhone or iPod Touch. What if you're away from your iTunes library and you want to listen to today's episode of National Public Radio's *Fresh Air* podcast?

Ah! Well, you can't synch the podcast into your iPhone's or iPod Touch's media library. But you *can* play it through your device "live," from the podcast's home server.

How? A podcast consists of two components on a server. There's the audio or video file that iTunes downloads from the server, and then there's (yes indeed) the RSS feed file that describes the content and helps iTunes (or any other podcatcher app) figure out that a new show has been uploaded.

So if you bookmark this podcast feed *directly*, you'll be able to play any podcast you want so long as you have a live Internet connection.

All you need to do is find the podcast or video podcast's RSS file and bookmark it in Safari. That's simple enough:

1. Find the show in your list of subscribed podcasts. In iTunes, choose Library ▶ Podcasts.

2. Right-click the title to bring up the item's pop-up menu. (If you're using a Mac with only one mouse button, you can bring up the pop-up menu by Control+clicking the title.) Make sure you right-click or Control+click on the title of the overall podcast, not on any individual episode.

3. Select Show Description from the pop-up menu. iTunes will open a little window describing the show. The URL for the podcast's RSS feed will be right at the top (see Figure 10-7).

If you want to use a podcast that you haven't subscribed to in iTunes, you'll have to do a Google search for the podcast's Web page. If you examine the page you should be able to spot an orange button that links to the feed. Tap this link on your iPhone or iPod Touch, and look at what happens: You wind up with a nice, RSS-y list of all the shows in the podcast (see Figure 10-8). Just choose an episode that seems interesting.

The actual online audio or video file associated with that episode is linked directly to the description (see Figure 10-9). Tap the little embedded Play button and, if it's a media type that the iPhone or iPod Touch can handle (and as the first syllable of the word "podcast" implies, that's almost a certainty), the video or audio will start streaming right from the server.

It works flawlessly. If you have a Wi-Fi connection to the Internet from your iPhone or iPod Touch, you can stream audio or video. But even if you're stuck with an AT&T EDGE cellular connection on the iPhone, you can still listen to audio just fine.

Safari's RSS capability is truly my kind of feature. It's nice to have something that's as muscular and well-articulated as the iTunes application, but it never does more for you than what Apple intended it to do. But a feature like RSS is so broad and powerful that it invites you to keep coming up with new ways to exploit it.

And as long as developers of Web sites and services keep coming up with new ways to incorporate feeds into the online world, Safari will continue to become more and more powerful and flexible.

11

Software, Kind Of (and No, Really)

The Skim

Fake Apps ■ Web-Based Software ■ Bookmarklets ■
Installing "Real" Non-Apple Apps ■ Securing Your iPhone ■
Tricky Today, Quaint Tomorrow?

She's become a legend among your circle of friends: an old friend's fiancée, a head chef who has been blessed with culinary gifts so keen that wildlife are routinely making the sixty-mile hike into the suburbs to ring her doorbell. "Word's gotten out," the steer and chickens and ducks and pigs explain. "If we're gonna be eaten anyway, we'd rather be served as something incredible than sold as part of a drive-through value meal."

You've been looking forward to the invitation for months, and it finally comes. It's not just *any* dinner, either: but Thanksgiving dinner for twelve! Seven courses!

"And you're coming on a good night," your pal enthuses. "Debbie's just started putting together a new special menu for the restaurant. So the *entire meal* will be meat-free! No dairy, either!"

How would you feel?

You'd still be looking forward to the meal, and (having dated a vegan myself, I can tell you that it'd probably still be one of the best dinners you've ever had). But still, when even the *possibility* of bacon has been removed from the event, a certain amount of disappointment is inevitable.

That's what happened to me about a month before the launch of the iPhone. Steve Jobs stood in front of thousands of software developers at Apple's annual programmers' conference and announced — with a smile on his face, no less — that the iPhone wouldn't support any third-party apps for the immediate future. Instead, all software produced outside of Apple would come in the form of "active" Web sites accessed via the browser, powered by Web technologies (see www.apple.com/webapps).

As it turned out, these online apps often look and perform just like "real" applications that live right on the device. But we want bacon, dammit.

The good news is that the online apps are useful. The better news is that even without any information or help from Apple, programmers have figured out how to write "real" iPhone software and install it on the device all the same. The state of these "real" third-party apps is in an incredible state of turbulence, but at least there are people out there fighting the good fight.

FAKE APPS

Oh, come on, Ihnatko. You're prejudicing this entire topic with a section title like that. Surely it's more appropriate to head this section with something like "Apple's officially supported iPhone apps, which aren't apps in the *truest* sense of the word because they're actually iPhone-specific Web pages that have been wired with enough smarts that they can often *feel* like 'real' apps."

Well, try fitting *that* on a page.

So don't let anyone tell you that Apple's "official" mechanism for outside software developers stinks. You hear, "It's actually a Web page" and that doesn't fill you with a lot of hope, but its mechanism is packed with protein:

- These special Web pages have sophisticated access to your device's features. They can incorporate parts of the iPhone user interface, dial phone numbers, and look up information that's stored on the device.
- They're not limited to static bits of information. The iPhone's browser understands JavaScript. It's like the Esperanto of languages for making Web pages behave like desktop software. So you can make an online iPhone app do some very sophisticated things.
- Safari also supports nearly every standard for Web design and includes a bunch of new standards that are specific to Web pages developed for the iPhone. So, developers can make an iPhone app look like whatever they want.
- iPhone apps will work with *any* device that runs that particular version of Safari. Meaning that every online app that was designed for the iPhone worked just fine for the iPod Touch the moment it was released. Cool!

Now, obviously, the size of the iPhone's screen means it'll be a long time before Microsoft will create a version of Excel for the iPhone that looks like the desktop version. But there's enough potential for the company to create an online articulation of that app that works great and makes perfect sense for a touch-based handheld.

(And actually, Microsoft doesn't have to. Because a company called EditGrid [www.editgrid.com] has created an astonishingly sophisticated Excel-compatible spreadsheet app that you can use straight from Safari. Try it out at iphone.editgrid.com.)

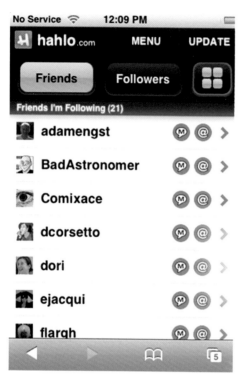

Figure 11-1
Hahlo, Cleveland! An example of an "online" app that's as good as a "real" app

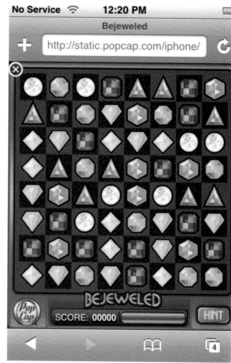

Figure 11-2
Bejeweled, sponsored by the long lines at the bank and the post office

Witness Figure 11-1. It's a rather nice iPhone or iPod Touch app called Hahlo (www.hahlo.com) that lets me read comments posted to the online Twitter service by my friends.

It's hard to imagine how this app would look any different if it "lived" on your iPhone instead of on a server at hahlo.com. It automatically hides Safari's address bar, so it doesn't look like a browser window. You have standard iPhone touch buttons, a list of items that scroll up and down but not side to side, and the same sort of interaction I have when I'm scrolling through a list of tracks in the music player app and choosing

individual items.

As a way of accessing an online service like Twitter, this sort of app is a natural. But holy cow, here's the classic PDA/phone game Bejeweled (see Figure 11-2). It's no doubt, no excuses, no "buts" the same animated and interactive puzzle game you'd be playing on a Treo or a Windows Mobile smartphone or any other handheld.

Like all online apps, there's no subscriptions, installation, or synching necessary. Just type the URL for the app into Safari (www.popcap.com for Bejeweled, as well as for other games from Popcap Studios) and you're there.

103

WEB-BASED SOFTWARE

Really, the selling point of online apps is that there's no selling involved at all. Plug a URL into Safari and you're using the app. If there's an online iPhone/iPod Touch app that requires that you tap in a credit card number first, I haven't heard of it.

So it's just up to you to *find* the damned things. But there are two swell resources:

◘ **iPhoneApplicationList**. There are a lot of online directories of iPhone/iPod Touch software, but iPhoneApplication-List (www.iphoneapplicationlist.com) is the one I rely on. It does tend to collect the newest software and they organize their listings into categories extremely well.

◘ **Leaflets**. This one has a big leg up on all others because it is, itself, an online iPhone app (see Figure 11-3). Put www. getleaflets.com into Safari and that's possibly the last application URL you'll even have to enter. The main screen is studded with buttons for a half-dozen useful little widgets but App List is the superstar. It presents you with a slick iPhone-y user interface and when you find an app you like, you can bookmark it into the device then and there without having to either retype the URL or add it to the list of desktop bookmarks that you synch to the phone. As with iPhoneApplicationList, the best selling point of Leaflets's App List is its organization. It features the three compulsories: a button to take you to the newest apps (so you can see what's fresh and exciting); a second button to take you to the most popular ones (which are likely to be high-quality and hugely useful apps); and a third button that takes you

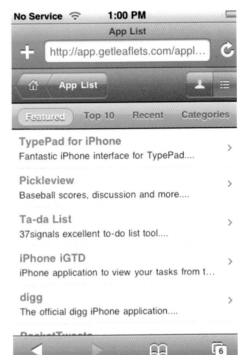

Figure 11-3
Leaflets is a wonderful concierge to the changing world of iPhone apps.

to a menu of nicely defined categories, so you can find precisely what you want.

BOOKMARKLETS

Good. By now you should be convinced that just because an app lives on a server instead of on your iPhone, that doesn't mean it isn't a fine piece of software that's worthy of love.

Still. You sort of wish you could put software *on* the device. It makes you feel real tough, like you could handle yourself in a fight or something.

A "bookmarklet" is a class of software that has some features of both. Remember what I said about JavaScript earlier? It's at the core

Figure 11-4
Bookmarklets put big, useful things in tiny little bookmarks.

javascript:x=escape(getSelection());if(!x)%7Bvoid
(x=prompt('%20Dictionary%20–%20Look%20
up:',''))%7D;window.location='http://dictionary.
reference.com/search?q='+x

See? That's actually a tiny program written in JavaScript. You can tap on it from your list of Safari bookmarks, only instead of opening a Web page, it pops up a little window (see Figure 11-4).

This is a bookmarklet that looks up words in an online dictionary. Type in a word — for technical reasons, Figure 11-4 was the best image I could generate, but I *would* have used a cool example word like "antidis-establishmentarianism" — and it'll open the appropriate word on Dictionary.com.

And bookmarklets aren't limited to just looking up Web pages. Safari is a wonderful browser, but it's missing a couple of basic features. Such as searching for a specific word in a long article. Welp, somewhere out there in the vast World Wide Web is a bookmarklet that'll highlight every instance of the word "propinquity" on the page.

Bookmarklets are saved as bookmarks on your local browser. On a desktop browser, that means trying out a bunch of bookmarklets on a great page like http://pimpmysafari.com/bookmarklets and then dragging the links to the ones you like into the bookmarks bar of your browser, or into its bookmarks manager.

But you can't drag links in the iPhone or iPod Touch edition of Safari. So you'll need to bookmark them using the default browser of whatever desktop machine your device synchs to. iTunes will copy the bookmarklet to your device.

Once it's there, you can move it into a special bookmarklets folder or any other place that makes sense to you.

of many of those iPhone apps. It's a whole programming language consisting of instructions that can be embedded into a Web page. When your browser loads the page, it sees the JavaScript and executes the instructions therein. "At this point," the Web page says, "I want you to check your internal clock for the correct date and slap 'Today's date is:' at this spot right here, followed by the date. Got that?"

A bookmarklet looks and behaves just like a Web bookmark. Only instead of a bookmark that looks like this:

http://pimpmysafari.com/bookmarklets

…it looks like this:

105

INSTALLING 'REAL' NON-APPLE APPS

If you know a nerd, geek, wonk, anorak, or any other sort of person who's usually the person with the greatest number of microprocessors on his body, in any room he enters, ... be *very very nice* to him. Because once a geek sets his mind on a goal (dammit), he doesn't let go of it until it's been reached.

"Wouldn't be *awesome* if we could land people on the Moon?"

"Why don't we?"

"Well, duh: because it'd cost forty billion dollars, probably."

"I got an uncle who works in the Kennedy White House. I bet *he* could convince someone to convince the president to convince the Congress to come up with forty billion."

"Really?"

"It's worth asking, wouldn't you say?"

And lo and behold, just nine years later, a threadbare space agency that hadn't even put a satellite into Earth orbit was broadcasting live video from the lunar surface.

As I said at the start of the chapter, Apple announced that (for now, anyway) the only way to write software for the iPhone and the iPod Touch is to do it as a Web-based app. To date, they've released *no* technical information, *no* programming tools, *no* examples, and *no* classware.

I mean, hell, there wasn't even a way to get a *file* onto the device unless it was piece of music, a video, or a photo and even then, you had to give it to iTunes first. A piece of functional software? Please.

The first working app appeared about two weeks after the iPhone went on sale. It did nothing but say, "Nyah nyah nyaaah, ... I'm a piece of software running on an iPhone"

Figure 11-5
You're not in Kansas any more with custom-installed iPhone apps.

(in so many words).

Today, some *remarkable* apps are available. They're clearly commercial-quality stuff, and although at this writing (three months after launch) it's still a bit of a black art, the field is getting better and richer with each passing week.

Don't believe me? Check out Figure 11-5, which shows the current state of my iPhone. I'm using a replacement for the standard Springboard iPhone application launcher, one that allows you to customize the screen. And whoah, nelly! The list of installed apps just keeps scrolling and scrolling.

In fact, this section of this chapter has

been tossed and rewritten twice already, and it got a desperate "*past* the last minute" addendum when Apple released a new firmware update that changed the game *again* three days after my final deadline.

The State of Third-Party iPhone Software

What's so frustrating about the situation is that Apple has been so damned ambivalent and vague about it. They haven't confirmed that "real" iPhone apps are *ever* coming.

You'd expect Apple to get into that business, or to at least turn the iTunes store into the official gatekeeper for third-party software. That is, it wouldn't be the Wild, Wild West (install any app from any source that performs any function), but there would be a way for a developer to write an app that the iPhone needs (like an outliner), submit it to Apple so they can see if it meets a certain standard for safety and quality, and then have it sold through the iTunes Store.

I'm still convinced that this will happen but again, Apple ain't talking.

And given how important this topic is, you'd think that they'd make some sort of statement explaining their policy. But no. A top Apple VP stated for the record that Apple had no particular beef against the big library of third-party apps that had been developed and published without any help from Apple. They wouldn't specifically do anything to make certain that future changes to the iPhone firmware and iTunes would remain compatible with them, but they wouldn't do anything to specifically eliminate them, either.

Annnnd then Apple released a firmware update that specifically eliminated them.

The state of the world today is this: There

are iPhones with firmware version 1.02 and earlier, which can run a fantastic library of commercial-grade (but free) third-party apps, and then there are the iPhones that run all later versions. Why's that? Because the firmware update that came after 1.02 made a fatal change to the way that an iPhone runs apps: Now, all apps must be "signed" by Apple. If an application doesn't have some sort of special mojo on it that tells the iPhone OS "Apple Incorporated has approved this application for use on this iPhone," it flat-out won't work.

But I remind you once again that software developers were able to figure out a way to write iPhone software from scratch, without a scrap of information or help from Apple. They'll figure out a way around this. Even now (literally two days after this fatal firmware update) developers have figured out ways to "rewind" an iPhone's firmware back to 1.02. Back to that magical land where you could install Tetris and book readers and instant-messaging clients, and drink purple tea from candy-colored teacups.

Details on installing apps in a post-1.02 world are still coming in at this writing. I mean, swear to God: The dudes who operate the printing press for this book are impatiently checking their watches and tapping their feet as I type this. For up-to-the-minute news, procedures, and information, I urge you to visit the following sites:

- http://iphone.fiveforty.net/wiki is the online clubhouse for iPhone third-party developers. It's very technical, but by necessity basic information on how to put apps on the device are always here.
- www.modmyiphone.com is the largest online community of people who are interested and engaged in modify-

TROUBLE

The installation instructions work just fine on an iPhone running version 1.02 of the iPhone firmware. These instructions aren't designed to work on the iPod Touch, but the development community is so upset about being torpedoed by Apple that I wouldn't be surprised if sometime in the coming year, it figured out a way to get apps running on *that* as well. So iPod Touch users should check out this section's URLs just the same.

But chiefly because I'm 100-percent certain that the development community will find a way around all of this, probably at first by creating a user-friendly app that "rewinds" your iPhone's firmware back to version 1.02. Way too much work, creativity, ingenuity, and passion has gone into developing the 1.02-and-earlier system for building third-party apps, and the community of developers and users don't seem to be interested in just shrugging their shoulders and going away.

Then developers will move onto dealing with the post-1.02 app challenge.

But that's speculation. Until Apple sanctions a method for outside developers to enhance and extend the iPhone, the mechanism for installing apps and the application library itself, described in the following sections, will continue to survive and even thrive.

Before, these developers were propelled by their intense curiosity and their desire to make their iPhones do cool thing. Now they're motivated by something even *more* powerful: spite. I was serious about what I said about the race to the Moon, but now's probably a good time to acknowledge that a lot of the USA's motivation to get there was knowing how angry the Russkies would be if we got there first.

ing their iPhones. Slightly more user-friendly than the preceding site, it has a big message board full of user experiences and tips.

- www.tuaw.com isn't specifically an iPhone resource. The Unofficial Apple Weblog has made it a priority to discuss iPhone techniques and has been all over the story of third-party development. And it's 100-percent a user-oriented site, so it's the least-scary resource of the three.

So if Apple has locked out third-party apps and (as of the day I write this) there's no working way to install them, why am I bothering to write about this?

Well, because it's an important issue. Even if a year from now it's still impossible to put "real" apps on your iPhone, I think it's interesting to see just how far developers got without any information from Apple, and how useful their apps actually were. It might make you a little bit mad that Apple didn't allow these people to continue working on behalf of the users.

Putting Real Apps on Your iPhone

And what a waste if third-party apps were to disappear. Setting up your 1.02-firmware iPhone so it'll run third-party apps isn't as easy as synching a collection of Steely Dan tracks to the device, but it's still well in reach of the average user.

It's still not a procedure for the squeamish. But if you've ever hooked up a DVD player, it's probably within your technical comfort zone. The only hairy part involves typing some old-fashioned text commands. Yes, on your iPhone. Holy cats!

One very simple and consumer-friendly app (available in both PC and Mac editions) does most of the work for you.

Figure 11-6
Installer: your first step into a larger world

First Part: on Your PC or Mac

Deep breath. Here we go. Once your iPhone's firmware has been rewound to version 1.02, as of this writing the third-party app installation procedure goes like this:

1. Visit http://iphone.nullriver.com and download either the Windows or the Mac edition of Installer.app. Install it on your computer as you would any other utility.

2. Connect your iPhone to your computer as normal, and wait until iTunes sees it, mounts it, and is done performing its automatic synch.

3. Run AppTapp Installer. The installer

handles the entire procedure from this point onward. It finds your iPhone attached via USB. It downloads a fresh copy of the iPhone's "personality" from Apple's own servers, establishes a connection to the iPhone, and installs the small piece of software that allows the Installer to install a much more complicated piece of software.

After the big software is locked and loaded, your iPhone will restart itself. If all went well, you'll see a brand-new application in the standard iPhone launcher: Installer (see Figure 11-6).

Installer is a Swiss Army-knife-kinda app. It lets you find new apps on the Internet, then it downloads them, installs them, and

TIP

If things go wrong, don't panic. If you don't wind up with a working copy of Installer on your iPhone, try installing Installer again (start again from Step 1).

Even the worst-case scenario is pretty mild. Just dock your iPhone and click the Restore button from the iPhone main settings screen. iTunes will restore your iPhone to its fresh-from-the-factory state and

an up-to-date (meaning: incompatible with third-party apps) version of the firmware. Many (but not all) of your settings will persist, and you won't have to sign up for a new account with your wireless provider.

The overwhelming consensus is that there's no way you can permanently damage your iPhone by using AppTapp Installer. Technically, it violates your warranty.

But don't be confused by what you might read elsewhere; there are other apps that are designed to "SIM-unlock" an iPhone (allow it to work on any cell phone network) and those are completely different things.

You *can* damage your phone with those SIM-unlock apps. But AppTapp won't break your phone.

TROUBLE

Are third-part apps safe?

Mmmmmmostly. You *should* be concerned.

A phone is a big, fat, tempting target for a no-goodnik. It's loaded with personal information (your address book, your passwords, your cell phone network info) and that's all valuable stuff to a criminal.

Secondly, there are ancient, but effective, scams where you set up a phone number in a faraway land that charges $100 per call, and trick a user into launching an app that calls the number.

Stuff like that. Installer. app helps you out by build-

ing a certain amount of "trustworthiness" into the system. If you're about to install an app the service has never heard of, published by someone they've never heard of, either, Installer will warn you.

Me, I don't install those apps. But as a rule of thumb, if Installer trusts an app, so do I.

---

lets you remove them if you're sick of 'em.

After Installer is up and running, you no longer need the desktop installer app and the iPhone doesn't need to be connected to your desktop via USB.

Second Step: on Your iPhone

You now have an app that can download and install *more* apps. When you tap on Install, it immediately takes you to a screen that looks for updated versions of third-party apps that have already been installed on your phone (see Figure 11-7).

"Out of the box," so to speak, Installer only looks for software that was built by the same people who built Installer itself. If you tap on the Sources tab, you can add additional software sources.

Installer will warn you that it can't vouch

Figure 11-7

The AppTapp Installer's opening screen

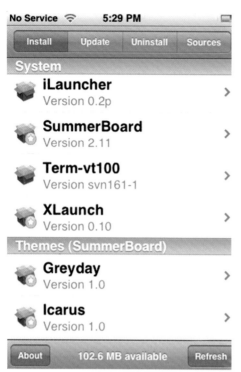

Figure 11-8
Installing SummerBoard, your first user app

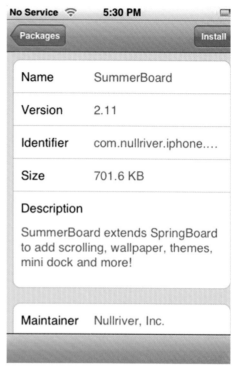

Figure 11-9
Details, details about a new app

for all sources. Fine, fine. But you'll need to approve this in order to get your mitts on the really cool stuff.

Your first download should be an app called SummerBoard. Or, actually, any app that allows the iPhone's built-in launcher app to scroll down and show additional applications.

Because, I mean, it would suck to have 20 additional apps on there but you can't launch 'em because they don't all fit on the main screen.

So let's use SummerBoard as an example of how to install more apps:

1. Tap Installer's Install button. A list of apps available for download appears

(see Figure 11-8). SummerBoard appears in the System category.

2. Tap SummerBoard. Installer will show you some information about the app (see Figure 11-9).

3. Tap the Install button, and then click Yes when asked to acknowledge that yup, you meant what you said. You'll see a couple of progress bars appear and, well, progress, as the application is first downloaded and then installed. SummerBoard is like a lot of System-level utilities in that it doesn't start working until you restart your iPhone. To complete installation, click on your phone's mechanical Home button.

Your iPhone will restart and Summer-Board will be ready to use.

Bit of a letdown, actually, because the whole point of SummerBoard is that it lets your list of application icons scroll and at the moment, you haven't added enough new apps to make scrolling necessary. But there's a *second* new app button, SMBPrefs, which lets you customize the look of the app launcher.

SECURING YOUR IPHONE

Before you do anything more — including "putting the iPhone back in your pocket and going out for dinner" — you need to perform an *absolutely essential* final step after installing these third-party apps on your iPhone.

The procedure for putting custom apps on your iPhone starts with a technique that's colloquially known as "jailbreaking." Jailbreaking is so easy because unlike just about all other smartphones, the iPhone runs the Unix operating system at its core. It's been around for decades and its ins and outs are well-understood by everybody.

So although Apple didn't provide a way for individual users to move arbitrary files onto an iPhones, geeks soon figured out that if you could use the standard USB connection to iTunes to sneak a common Unix networking app onto the iPhone, then that one little app would throw the door to the iPhone wide open.

That little app allows any computer on the Wi-Fi network to log in to the iPhone and give it commands and copy files into it. Or read files off of it. Or do just about everything.

Scary!

Oh, wait: You'd need to know the hardware address of the iPhone. Plus, you'd have to know the iPhone's super-secret Apple-assigned password.

No, wait, go with your first impulse to be scared. If you've jailbroken your iPhone and you're sitting in a Starbucks with the thing right in your pocket, here's what I could do from *my* iPhone:

1. I use Secret Utility Number 1 to "sniff" the air and get a list of all active Wi-Fi devices nearby. After a quick guess, I have your phone's network address.

2. I use Secret Utility Number 2 to ask your iPhone to log into its operating system. It obediently asks for a user-name and password.

3. I type in the phone's username and password. I know what it is … because *every iPhone has the exact same system password.*

4. And now I can look at all your photos and e-mails and download any ones I find interesting. Just for starters. I have access to the whole thing. If you're lucky, I'll just destroy your iPhone data and render it temporarily inoperative.

You're outraged. I can sense that. Go get a glass of water and calm down and then come back.

Okay. You're wondering why Apple assigned the same password to every iPhone? Well, why not? They didn't include any software that makes the iPhone even the slightest bit vulnerable to invasions. *You* did that, Mr. (or Ms.) Genius! Blithely following advice you got out of some stupid *book* and not knowing that the author failed to warn you about these things!

Calm down, calm down …. I'm warning you right now. And in the next bit, I'm going to tell you how to change the passwords on your iPhone to make it almost completely invulnerable.

(Yes, "almost." Because changing the passwords doesn't prevent someone from finding and attempting to log into your iPhone. It just means that they'll have no idea what the password is. If you choose something clever like "password" for your password, the weasel will probably be in after two or three tries.)

Here we go again. You'll need to change the passwords on *two* built-in user accounts. Don't worry, neither of these have anything to do with the normal operation of your iPhone. All you're doing is nailing shut a couple of long-forgotten service entrances.

To do this, you'll need to download and install two software packages, using Installer.

1. Locate and install BSD Subsystem and MobileTerminal. You'll find them both listed under System. BSD Subsystem adds a bunch of low-level commands to the iPhone's Unix OS, including the command for changing passwords. MobileTerminal allows you to access your iPhone's OS and give it those low-level commands

2. Press the Home button to get to your iPhone's app launcher. Tap Mobile Terminal. Oh, horror! An old-fashioned Seventies-era green-on-black terminal (see Figure 11-10)! Yup, it's scary, but you've got some simple stuff to do. First, you need to change the iPhone's "master" account password. The account's name is "root."

3. Using the onscreen keyboard, type "passwd root" (without the quotes) and then tap the Return key. Type carefully; it's not easy to go back and change mistakes with this terminal app.

4. Through that funky green text, the iPhone's Unix OS will ask you to type a new password. Again, type *carefully*. For

Figure 11-10

A must-do step: changing the passwords on your iPhone

safety's sake, the iPhone will ask you to type the new password again, just to make sure you didn't make a typo without knowing it. Choose a password that folks aren't likely to guess. Mind you, you'll probably never ever have to use this password ever again. But it's always *possible* that in the future, there'll be an unknown new app that lets you do something useful with this remote login feature. If that happens, you'll be happy that you didn't just type some random numbers and letters. The iPhone will change its password and then obediently return to Unix's

prompt, letting you know that it's ready for a new command. Now it's time to change the password on the iPhone's second built-in account.

5. Type "passwd mobile" but again, no quotes. Repeat what you did in Step 4.

You're done. Both doors have now been secured.

Now go off and have fun. An iPhone with third-party apps is a wonderful, wonderful thing. By far the biggest advantage is that you have tools that will work even on an airplane or in upper Vermont or any other place where you can't access the Internet, and thus can't access any online apps.

Oh, and there are games. Let's not downplay games. I like games.

TRICKY TODAY, QUAINT TOMORROW?

Once again I think I deserve your pity and compassion. Over the life of this book project, writing this apps chapter and making sure it's as up-to-date and valuable as possible has felt like being dragged over a gravel road by a horse that knew I wasn't wearing my steel-plated pants that day. I know that the chapter isn't entirely about third-party apps, but it's by far the most fascinating part of the iPhone experience and it demands that I write about it.

It's October 2007 and this book is now seconds away from being locked down. I don't know if a year from today, the "third party apps" section will be useful, basic information, or a quaint nostalgic look back at a simpler and more innocent time, like an all-day marathon of *Who's the Boss?* on cable.

So let's go back to those days when Steve Jobs announced that there'd be no third-party apps for the iPhone. I was disappointed, but I really should have known better. Apple set a very nice table with those Web apps. But sure enough, when you take the ham and the turkey out of a Thanksgiving dinner, you can count on *somebody* sneaking a bag of take-out barbecue into the place.

12

Sticking Web Pages in Your Ear

The Skim

The Right Tool: iNewsCaster ∎ iNewsCaster and iTunes

One of the pleasures and one of the daily banes of my job is that I have to keep on top of lots of different news sites and blogs. This is all interesting stuff I'm reading (well, most of it, anyway) and it's great that something I would have been doing anyway is, in fact, part of my job description.

Spiffy. But all the same, it means that there are way too many occasions when someone sees me lying on the sofa with my feet propped up, a cool drink at my elbow, and a notebook balanced on my stomach, and he or she is openly skeptical when I say, "But I *am* working." The banes of the self-employed are the friends and relatives who will try to guilt you into taking their kids for the day when there's a snow day or something. Parrying off the selfish invasions of these interlopers requires ceaseless vigilance, and the sight of me on my sofa with Cheeto's dust on my nonmousing hand really doesn't help me.

It's a good idea to jump in the car for a road trip from time to time. After all, a neighbor can't drop off little Tralfaz if I'm somewhere along the 113-mile route between my house and this little diner in Bellows Falls, Vermont. And if I'm spending those two hours listening to Web sites that I've converted into spoken text, when the neighbor calls me on my iPhone I can say, "But I *am* working" then, too.

With news and information being sweetly and synthetically spoken through the car speakers, I can truly live the dream of productivity and avoidance.

THE RIGHT TOOL: INEWSCASTER

MagneticTime (www. magnetictime.com) makes a swell utility called iNewsCaster, available for both PC and Mac. You can download a free trial from their Web site; if you want to keep it, it's thirty bucks.

iNewsCaster is like Bloglines or Google Reader (which I talked about in Chapters 9 and 10): It converts blog and news site articles into spoken text through the sites' syndication feeds. These feeds are little database files that contain information about everything that's been posted, and when.

By monitoring these feeds every fifteen minutes or so, the app can automatically download newly published text and add it to its library. When you're ready to convert your Web content to speech, you just click on the headlines that seem interesting and then iNewsCaster does the rest.

The Windows Edition

Figure 12-1 shows iNewsCaster's main window for its Windows version. As you can see, the app has been busy, grabbing headlines from a bunch of different sources.

You can add sites to iNewsCaster's watch list with just a few clicks:

1. Click the Add Feeds button, located in the Common Tasks pane of the main window. iNewsCaster's Settings window opens (see Figure 12-2).

2. Scroll the pane on the left until you

Figure 12-1
iNewsCaster's news harvest

see the News Feeds section. A bunch of popular news feeds are built in, organized by category. Just click the checkbox of any feed that you'd like iNewsCaster to watch for you. You can also add the feeds of your favorite sites and blogs manually. To do that, ...

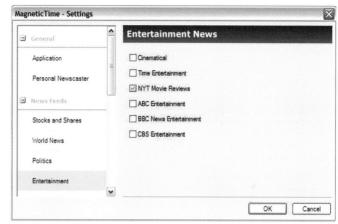

Figure 12-2

Adding newsfeeds to iNewsCaster via its built-in feed library

3. Scroll the list down to the very last item and click Custom Feeds.

4. Click the Add button. A dialog box appears.

5. Paste the URL to your favorite site's newsfeed into the dialog and click OK (see Figure 12-3). Repeat for each custom site and blog. Turn once again to Chapters 9 and 10 for tips on how to locate the URL for a site's newsfeed.

iNewsCaster will automatically check each of your subscribed feeds for new content, and download any fresh articles it finds. When you want to convert these articles to spoken audio files:

1. Click the checkboxes of all the articles that seem

interesting enough that you'd like to listen to them in the car or during your morning run.

2. Click the iPod button at the top-right corner of the screen (see Figure 12-4).

3. That's it; iNewsCaster will start grinding down all the articles into spoken text.

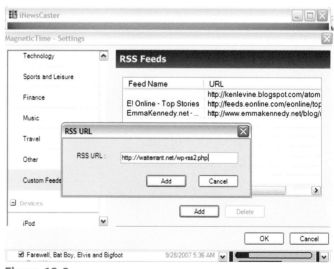

Figure 12-3

Adding a feed of your own

Figure 12-4
The magical button to start the conversion process going

The Mac Edition

The Mac version of iNewsCaster operates in nearly the same way as the Windows edition. The layout of the buttons is just a little bit different (see Figure 12-5).

Some things to note:

▶ To add subscriptions, click the Add Feeds button at the bottom of the window. This will open the app's Preferences window, through which you can select feeds

that have already been wired into iNews-Caster and add feeds of your own.

▶ To convert feeds into audio files, select articles of interest from the list and then click the Export button.

INEWSCASTER AND ITUNES

No matter which app you use, the result is the same: a pile of very natural-sounding spoken-text files in iTunes, ready to be synched to your iPhone or iPod Touch.

The files will automatically be added to a new playlist called iNewsCaster. The app also identifies the tracks' artist as iNewsCaster, so it's easy to build smart playlists that automatically load (for example) just the most recent ten converted tracks that have a run-

Figure 12-5
iNewsCaster for Macintosh

TIDBIT

Despite iNewsCaster's strengths, you might sometimes be disappointed when using it: You're eagerly settling in, expecting to have all *New York Times* film reviews read to you, but all you hear are brief summaries!

Well, that's not iNewsCaster's fault. Not all feeds contain the entire text of the article. Some sites prefer that you use feedreader software just to see what's new and interesting. If you want to read the article, they want you to visit the actual site, where you might be tempted to read other articles and maybe click on some ads. So their site feed only contains article summaries.

documents and other desktop items in ways that ensure they'll always be available to you — Internet connection or no — work just dandy with Web pages, too.

ning time of more than five minutes.

It seems a bit weird to be devoting a chapter to the mystical and arcane practice of carrying Web pages around on a device that has a perfectly functional connection to the Internet and a kick-butt browser. But building "robo-podcasts" of your favorite sites adds a different spin to how you get your information from the Web.

And don't let this be the end of your explorations. It's great that the iPhone and the iPod Touch have Internet connections, but you can't always count on those connections being available to you (particularly if you have an iPod Touch, which always depends on the kindness of strangers (viz: open Wi-Fi access points) for Internet access.

Be sure to turn to Chapter 19 for more tips. That chapter's techniques for converting

13

Podcasts

The Skim

Here's a spoiler alert, in case you haven't figured it out yet: The basic purpose of the Internet is to provide hundreds of thousands of jerks, dweeks, geeks, freaks, flakes, egotists, ignoramuses, nut jobs, loners, twits, arrogant pinheads, and delusional Travis Bickle aficionados a way to share their unique articulations of individual insanity with a potential audience of millions of total strangers.

Podcasting was invented when members of the above group realized that the human population could insulate themselves from these messages by simply sealing themselves inside a metal automobile or any other place where you can't read text.

Still, as podcasting became part of mainstream communication, the level of content available via podcast was raised. Now, the same shows you tune in to all the time on public radio, local stations, and national TV networks can arrive on your desktop (and thence your iPhone or iPod Touch) at regular intervals at no charge.

I should warn you that the folks who podcast from major networks and the like are (generally speaking) no less stable or egotistical than the Internet freelancers. But at least you know they're probably making a comfortable living. A full belly tends to stifle baser urges to inflict stress

Figure 13-1
Your first step into a larger world

and mayhem upon society.

PODCAST BACKGROUND

Podcasts combine all the best technologies and infrastructures of the Internet in ways that you, the user, can safely ignore:

- Somewhere in the world, someone sits down with a microphone and records a show. She uploads it to a server somewhere on the Internet.

- The Internet server contains a little file that keeps track of each episode. It contains a description of the podcast and a synopsis of each individual episode. And, most important for your purposes, there's a record of what date and time the show was first posted to the server.

- iTunes periodically checks this file because you've told iTunes that you like this show. It's *called* a subscription but not to worry: It's free, free, free. iTunes automatically downloads new episodes as they appear and adds them to your iTunes library.

- And because you've also told iTunes to automatically copy new podcasts to your iPhone or your iPod Touch, each morning when you take the device from its desktop dock and toss it into your car, your morning commute is filled

with fresh content that (a) appeared from thin air without your having done anything at all and, thrillingly, (b) didn't cost you a penny.

Apart from the "it doesn't cost you a penny" thing, the second-most-thrilling thing about podcasts is that the content is controlled by the same fundamental prin-

Figure 13-2
The front doors of the iTunes Podcast Directory

ciple that guides *all* the content that you encounter on the Internet, viz:

On the Internet, nobody can hear you ask, "But what's the point of this, really?"

Which means that there's a truly dizzying array of content available. Any jerk with a $10 microphone and a two-bit opinion has the same access to the speakers in my office as any of the Big Four networks. So during your morning commute, it's entirely possible

Figure 13-3
iTunes's Top Podcasts: It's all a popularity contest.

over the world, and it's available to me any time I want to hear it. As opposed to radio, which limits me to whatever happens to be on whatever station I happen to be able to receive in whatever city I happen to be in.

(Think about your least-favorite national radio personality. I mean, come on, do you *really* think he'd have a career if listeners had any choice in the matter?)

There's a three-pronged approach to filling your iPhone with podcasts:

that you'll be listening to last night's polished, professional, and highly illuminating broadcast edition of *ABC News: Nightline*. Then you move to the next podcast, which is a heavy-metal show by some guy named Jason from Salt Lake City who's complaining about how he got this *awesome* Motorhead tattoo on his back but now feels cheated because he's the only person who never gets to actually *see* it.

When iTunes started supporting podcasts, it totally changed the way I used portable players like the iPhone. And (oh, dear) at the time, it completely killed any remaining interest I had in traditional, broadcast radio. I get the best programming from all

1. Locate a podcast that seems at least 38 percent interesting.
2. Tell iTunes to subscribe to that podcast.
3. Configure your iPhone to automatically load new episodes as they land in your iTunes library.

FINDING PODCASTS IN THE ITUNES STORE

Apple maintains a huge and fairly ginchy searchable directory of podcasts, and you can access it straight from iTunes.

The iTunes Podcast Directory

To visit the iTunes Podcast Directory, choose Sources ▶ Podcasts in iTunes and then click the Podcast Directory button in the lower-right corner of the window (see Figure 13-1).

Click the Go to Podcast Directory button to proceed. You'll quickly be connected to the entrance to the iTunes Podcast

Figure 13-4
Featured news podcasts

Directory (see Figure 13-2).

The iTunes Podcast Directory lives on one of Apple's servers on the Internet, not on your own hard drive. So you'll need to have a live connection to the Internet in order to access the thing.

Figure 13-5
Podcast cat-
egories on
the directory's
front page

And at this point you should regard yourself as not unlike young Charlie Bucket in *Willy Wonka and the Chocolate Factory*. No, not the Johnny Depp movie, the *good* one, the one which has a scene where the kids get to run through a little park made entirely out of candy and sample to their hearts' delight.

Obviously there's lots of eye-candy at the front door. Individual podcasts get front-row attention, usually because they're new or suddenly hot. But your first clicks should probably go to the Top Podcasts list (see Figure 13-3). It's a ranking based on popularity, which almost always means that they're well-produced shows with terrific content, and new episodes come out regularly.

Your next focus is in the center of the window: the big, colorful category buttons. Click one of these, and iTunes will take you to a selected assortment of featured podcasts related to the category (see Figure 13-4).

Why *these* podcasts and not others? Because they're all produced with a professional attitude (even if they weren't necessarily produced by professional broadcasters) and are both popular and regularly updated. But by no means should you conclude that there are only 100 news podcasts in the directory. To see the entire list, return to the main directory (just click the Back button at the top of the directory window;

it works just like a Web browser) and feast your eyes on the Categories list (see Figure 13-5).

Click any one of these category names and you'll be taken to the front page of that particular category, which will have its own Featured Podcasts and Top Podcasts lists.

Incidentally, iTunes's main search feature (that big Search box at the upper-right corner of the iTunes window) will search the Podcast Directory as well as the music store. So if you know precisely what you're looking for — and you don't mind sifting through a bunch of music tracks that also match your search query — you'll save a couple of steps.

Again I cite the Fundamental Principle of the Internet: Apple isn't interested in stopping people from making their podcasts widely available, so if the podcaster submits the show's URL to Apple and there are no legal issues involved, they'll add the podcast with little ado. So you'll find lots and lots and *lots* of noise, with a few gems mixed in.

	Name		Artist		Album	
1	For Political Junkies Only	⊕	WBZ		For Political Junkies Only	⊕
2	WBZ NewsRadio Headlines	⊕	WBZ NewsRadio 1...		WBZ NewsRadio Headlines	⊕
3	WBZ's Inside The Clubhouse!	⊕	WBZ		WBZ's Inside The Clubhou...	⊕
4	WBZ's News Makers	⊕	WBZ		WBZ's News Makers	⊕
5	WBZ Sports	⊕	WBZ NewsRadio 1...		WBZ Sports	⊕
6	WBZ's Carl Stevens Online Journal	⊕	WBZ		WBZ's Carl Stevens Onlin...	⊕
7	WBZ Bruins Audio	⊕	WBZ NewsRad... ⊕		WBZ Bruins Audio	⊕
8	WBZ's More on This...	⊕	WBZ		WBZ's More on This...	⊕
9	WBZ Sports	⊕	WBZ NewsRad... ⊕		WBZ Sports	⊕
10	The Garden Guru	⊕	WBZ NewsRad... ⊕		The Garden Guru	⊕

Figure 13-6
Searching for WBZ podcasts

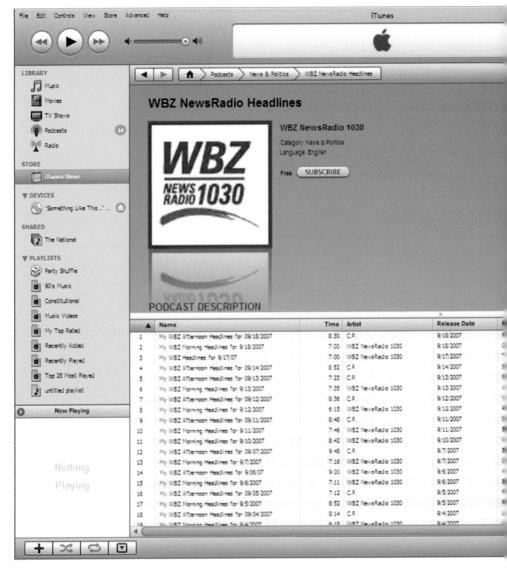

Figure 13-7
Looking at a podcast

The Featured Podcasts lists and the iTunes Store's Search box are far more useful than scanning through thousands and thousands of individual podcasts.

I mentioned earlier that I don't listen to radio any more. I *do* listen to radio *shows*, however. Hmmm. I wonder if any of my local radio stations here in Boston have interesting podcasts?

It's easy enough to find out. iTunes can

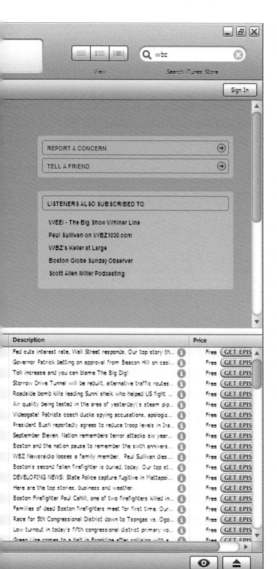

Figure 13-8
The Subscribe button

of interest, you can find out more about the show by clicking its little square poster image (if it's a featured podcast) or the circular arrow button next to its title (if it turned up in a search or some other listing). iTunes will take you to the podcast's main directory listing (see Figure 13-7).

You'll find a description of the podcast, a list of all the shows available at the moment, and possibly some user comments. Clicking the Web site link will open the show's official Web site in your Web browser. Double-click an individual episode (or use its Get Episode button) to download that episode immediately and listen to it in iTunes.

Subscribing to Podcasts through the iTunes Directory

If you've spent some time noodling through the Directory, you've spotted Subscribe buttons here and there (see Figure 13-8). Yes indeed, this button does precisely what you think it does. Click it, and iTunes will subscribe you to that podcast. It'll start off by downloading the latest episode and adding it to your personal iTunes library. And from that point onward, iTunes will automatically download new episodes. That's all there is to it.

OTHER PODCAST DIRECTORIES

Apple didn't invent the concept of pod-

search for any word that appears in the podcast listing: people, topics, places, anything. I'll just pop the call letters of local radio and TV station WBZ into a search. Witness the result (see Figure 13-6).

Learning More about a Podcast

No matter how you hit upon a podcast

casting, as neat as the iTunes Podcast Directory is. They don't own the concept, either. Nobody does. So there are plenty of podcasts available that don't appear in the iTunes directory.

But honestly, if you eagerly download a show that doesn't appear in the iTunes Directory, be prepared to have your heart broken. Getting listed in iTunes is (a) free, (b) a simple, well-documented procedure, and (c) a fairly automatic approval from iTunes, unless you're doing something naughty, like explaining how to sneak an old Band-Aid into a bottle of beer and seal it up again to make it look as though it came from the factory that way so you can maybe scam a free case out of your local liquor store.

I find that the biggest advantage of the alternative directories is that they highlight different shows and organize their content a little differently. Which means that there's a good chance there's a terrific podcast buried deep inside iTunes where I'll never find it, but which I'll trip over on Odeo by accident.

Some swell podcast directories:

- ◘ **Odeo**. It's very iTunes-like (www.odeo. com). It's well organized by categories which makes it easy to spot the popular and most heavily-updated podcasts.
- ◘ **Podcast.net**. This is a good'n chiefly because it's so exhaustive (www.podcast. net). Which is also its weakness. I'm not particularly interested in learning about *every* technology podcast that's ever been published, I just want to find a couple of *good* ones. But it's great for casting a wide net.
- ◘ **Podcastalley**. A strong front page (www.podcastalley.com). It's a directory, but it's also backed by lots of info *about* podcasts and podcasters. Another one

of those directories that's excellent for discovering a podcast you'd never heard of about a topic you didn't think you'd be interested in, which nonetheless becomes one of your can't-miss shows.

- ◘ **DigitalPodcast**. A generalized directory with good social features (www. digitalpodcast.com) such as recommending podcasts to friends and reading user comments.
- ◘ **Del.icio.us**. It's not actually a podcast directory, but this directory of sites (http://del.icio.us) tagged by millions of Internet users is a good resource for finding stuff on the Web that other people have recommended. Search for "podcast" plus any topic words and you'll probably come across a bunch of podcasts that folks liked so much that they wanted to remember them.

SUBSCRIBING TO A PODCAST MANUALLY

Naturally, subscribing to a podcast you discovered without the help of the iTunes Podcast Directory, or just by browsing around the Web, isn't as simple as clicking a friendly Subscribe button.

Umm, unless the podcast has a friendly "Subscribe to this podcast in iTunes" button or link. It might incorporate some flavor of the icon in Figure 13-9, which is Apple's own special "this is a link to a podcast" button. It might just explicitly say, "Subscribe with iTunes."

Or, something else entirely. The thing is, these people who create Web pages are all mavericks. They're wild stallions, unbroken, untamed; they may bend your precious rules but dammit, they get the job done. Et cetera.

But it isn't terribly complicated. Remember earlier, when I told you that every podcast is represented by a simple file somewhere on the Internet? All you need to do is give iTunes the address of that file.

I apologize in advance for this, but I am forced to introduce a technical three-letteracronym into the proceedings.

That three-letter acronym is RSS. It's the simple, worldwide standard that powers podcasts (and weblogs and all sorts of Internet services). Technically, the address you're hunting for is known as an "RSS feed." For instance, Figure 13-10 shows you the RSS link for Fanboy Radio. It's a podcast intended for consumption by geeks, so needless to say they've included their podcast links in the geekiest way possible. And why not? Their audience (comic book fans — my people) groks that sort of thing.

In this case, the colored button that reads RSS 2.0 attracts our full and immediate attention. It represents a link to the RSS feed we want to give to iTunes. It also says, "Syndication," which is another tipoff that it's a link to the podcast feed. "Feed," "XML," and "iPod" are other triggers.

To copy the link:

1. Right-click the link. (If you're using a Macintosh with a one-button mouse, Control+click the link.)

2. Select Copy Link or Copy Link Location (depending on which Web browser you're using).

And that's it. I deliberately chose a pretty awful example but not to worry: Most podcast Web pages put that RSS feed link way out in the open. Figure 13-11 shows you the RSS link for a National Public Radio show. I mean, *now* we're talkin'. The URL is explicitly pointed out to you *and* there's a direct iTunes button. Behold, Your Tax Dollars,

Working For *You*.

After you've copied the link to the podcast's RSS feed, just hand it off to iTunes:

1. Choose Advanced ▶ Subscribe to Podcast.

2. Paste the URL into the text box and click OK (see Figure 13-12).

Figure 13-9

Apple's own little podcast icon; clicking this icon on a Web page might subscribe you to a podcast.

Figure 13-10

Hunting for a podcast's RSS feed: target sighted

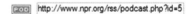

Figure 13-11

A less-cruel display of a podcast's RSS feed

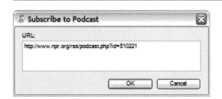

Figure 13-12

Manually subscribing to a podcast

Figure 13-13
A glorious cornucopia of free content

And from that point onward. iTunes treats the podcast the same as it would if you'd found it in the iTunes directory. It'll add the podcast to your list of subscriptions, download the most recent episode, and then download future shows as they're published.

MANAGING SUBSCRIPTIONS

You can see all the podcasts you've subscribed to by clicking Library ▶ Podcasts in the iTunes Library (see Figure 13-13).

If iTunes knows that there are episodes that it hasn't downloaded — for instance, it's a new subscription, which would mean that iTunes only downloaded the latest show — you can manually download it by clicking the little Get button next to its title.

If there's an exclamation point (!) to the left of the podcast's title (note "Penn Radio Archive" and "NPR: My Cancer" in Figure 13-13) it means there was a problem when trying to update that item. Either the server where the audio files live isn't available, or the podcast has been discontinued, or perhaps the Universe doesn't believe that you're one of those people who deserve to have nice things happen to them.

Updating a Podcast Manually

By default, iTunes will automatically look for new episodes of your podcasts on a regular basis. If you want iTunes to look *right freaking now* — you're about to leave the house for a three-hour drive to your folks' house and you don't want to be 18 minutes in before you realize that you've already heard everything on your iPhone — just click the Refresh button in the lower-right corner of the iTunes window. Make sure you're looking at your list of podcasts first; if you're looking at your music library, that button will say and do something else entirely.

iTunes will update all your subscriptions immediately, automatically downloading any new shows that you don't already have. If you'd like to update just one show, choose Update Podcast from the podcast's contextual menu (right-click or Control+click the

podcast's name). Only that one podcast will be updated.

Unsubscribing

If at some point in life you discover that *Shawn and Kyle's Super-Awesome Weekly Movie Hurl* podcast is neither weekly, nor is it consistently about movies, and "barely adequate" is a stretch, let alone "Super-Awesome," you can unsubscribe to the podcast by clicking its title and then clicking the Unsubscribe button at the lower-left corner of the iTunes window.

CHANGING HOW PODCASTS ARRIVE IN ITUNES

The lower-left corner also sports a Settings button, which is where you tell iTunes how it should manage all your podcasts as a group (see Figure 13-14).

You can also access podcast settings through iTunes's Preferences panel (choose Edit ▶ Preferences in Windows and iTunes ▶ Preferences on the Mac).

Here, you can tell iTunes how frequently it ought to update your podcasts, and what it should do with them after you've got 'em. Through the Check for New Episodes pop-up menu, you can

Figure 13-14
The Podcasts options let you tell iTunes how it should update your podcasts.

tell iTunes to check hourly, daily, weekly, or manually. Manually means that it's entirely up to you to remember to click iTunes's Update button and check for new episodes.

And what should iTunes do when it finds new content? When New Episodes Are Available offers three choices:

▸ **Download All** grabs every episode you

don't have. If *The Jeff Boring McDullsworth Show* has 230 half-hour episodes available, then iTunes is downloading all 230.

▸ **Download the most recent one** does what it says. It assumes that you're not, you know, obsessive-compulsive about this sort of thing and you just

Figure 13-15
Deciding how podcasts wind up on your iPhone

want whatever's newest. But iTunes will kindly grab all the information about the shows it didn't download, and add the info to the podcast's program listings so you can peruse them at your leisure.

◪ **Do nothing** seems like a waste of a good resource. But at least it's fairly easy to understand. Instead of downloading any new episodes, iTunes will simply add information about those episodes to your subscription listing.

After iTunes updates your podcast subscriptions, the new content will be snug and secure in your iTunes library, and any info about shows that it didn't download will appear in the listing.

CHANGING HOW PODCASTS ARRIVE ON YOUR IPHONE OR IPOD TOUCH

The final thing in iTunes's Podcasts settings window is iPhone Preferences (or iPod Preferences on the iPod Touch). This button takes you straight to the Podcasts settings panel of your iPhone's (or iPod Touch's) preferences page (see Figure 13-15). You won't see this unless the device is plugged into your computer.

By default, iTunes selects Automatically Update All Unplayed Podcasts for you. Every podcast that appears in iTunes will automatically be copied into your device, where they'll appear in its built-in podcasts list.

Fabulous. This works peachy-keen if you have a modicum of self-control and don't subscribe to more podcasts than your poor little 4- (8-, 16-) gigabyte device can handle.

Otherwise, you're quickly going to run of space on your iPhone or iPod Touch. Picture yourself in the car, laughing merrily at the

acres of bumper-to-bumper traffic. There is a song in your heart because a two-hour delay gives you all the time in the world to listen to a recent podcast you downloaded which features three hours with the creators of *The Matrix*, in which they admit that the first movie was sort of okay but then the final two were just self-indulgent, pretentious nonsense and then they invite people just like you to punch them each in the sternum once.

And then you discover that none of it got copied to your iPhone because everything you've downloaded over the past week had left it filled to capacity.

So clearly, it's a Good Thing to allow iTunes to be a bit more selective about the content it sends to your device. Automatically Update Selected Podcasts Only lets you point-and shoot just a handful of podcasts that should always be automatically updated, leaving the rest behind. Click the checkboxes of those podcasts you just can't live without.

As for the Manually Manage Podcasts option, well, that's no fun, obviously. iTunes won't automatically copy shows to your iPhone but instead will leave that task completely up to you.

Bummer.

Truth be told, though, that's what I've selected in *my* iTunes library. Those automatic features are terrific because they don't require any heavy lifting at all, but the cost is that you cede a lot of control. If you become even slightly adept at iTunes and how to manage playlists, you can easily set up iTunes to copy podcasts precisely the way you like 'em, by organizing them into smart playlists.

For example, Figure 13-16 shows a smart playlist I set up that always ensures that the newest podcasts land on my iPhone. The

TIDBIT

Be sure to turn to Chapter 10 for one of my favorite iPhone/iPod Touch tricks. Your device has a connection to the Internet, so it *should* be able to download new podcasts straight from the ether, right? Alas, Apple didn't include that feature. But by bookmarking the podcast's RSS feed in Safari, you can have the latest episode streamed through your iPhone or iPod Touch, directly from the server. Chapter 10 has all the colorful language and pictures explaining how this works.

tening to podcasts is this smart playlist, and after you've heard the latest *Martini Shot*, the iPhone starts playing the newest *SmodCast* because it's the next item in the playlist. Hours and hours of uninterrupted music and nobody has to die. That sounds like a pretty fair deal to me.

For more information on building and using smart playlists, the Library of Congress (actually, just me) recommends Chapter 2 of this very same book.

Podcasting is such a wonderful thing that it's utterly *astounding* that you humans haven't discovered a way to wreck it yet. A world full of free, rich content that lands on your iPhone as though delivered by pixies while the shoemaker slept. I've been at this since there were less than 500 podcasts in the world and I'm still amazed by the content.

Hey, here's a tip: Search for "magnatune" in the iTunes podcast directory. It's a music publisher with a freaky way of doing business: It hosts dozens and dozens of regular podcasts featuring recordings from its library. An hour of Mozart, every week. Or Bach. Or jazz. Or Xanthanian typewriter-swallowing music. No ads, no cuts, no commercials; it's like a public radio station used to be.

The idea is that if you like some of the music in the podcast, maybe you'll visit www.magnatune.com and buy some of it on CD. I should, um, probably do that sometime.

It's also slightly remarkable that Apple is the one maker of portable devices that supports podcasting so aggressively. Just think for a moment: Apple makes jillions of dollars a year by selling people content through the iTunes Store. And yet they use that same entity's massive resources to connect their customers to hundreds of thousands of hours

first line says, "This playlist should only contain podcasts." The second makes sure that the podcast will be removed from the playlist automatically after I've heard it, and replaced with fresh content.

The playlist always contains 50 podcasts, and iTunes always fills any open slots with the most recently added podcasts.

The end result is a playlist on my iPhone that always contains the newest 50 unheard podcasts. And there's an added boon. Normally, when the iPhone or iPod Touch reaches the very end of a podcast, it stops playback and returns you to the podcasts list. Which means that you're hurtling down I-95 at 70 miles an hour with nothing but dead air in the car. Unless you reach over, take your eyes off the road and a hand off the wheel, and make another selection. But you'd never do *that*, of course, so your only alternative is to jerk the steering wheel and crash into a bridge abutment, ending your pain quickly.

But when your normal mechanism for lis-

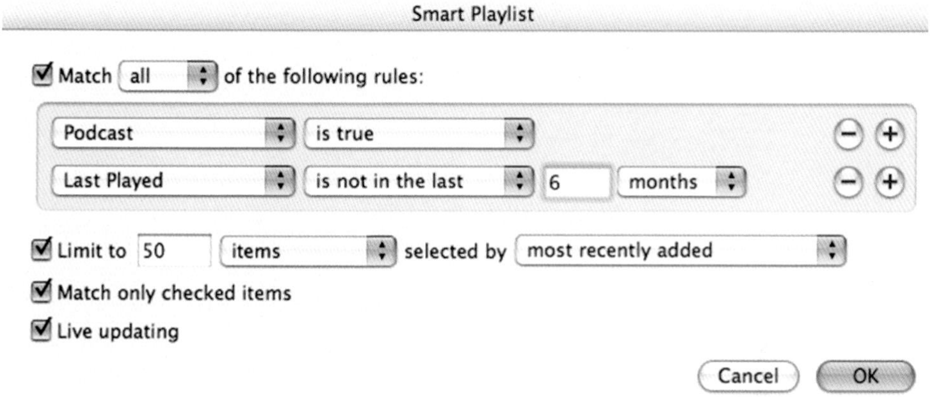

Smart Playlist

☑ Match [all ⬍] of the following rules:

| [Podcast ⬍] | [is true ⬍] | | ⊖ ⊕ |
| [Last Played ⬍] | [is not in the last ⬍] | [6] [months ⬍] | ⊖ ⊕ |

☑ Limit to [50] [items ⬍] selected by [most recently added ⬍]
☑ Match only checked items
☑ Live updating

(Cancel) (OK)

Figure 13-16
Taking greater control over iPhone content with smart playlists

of free content. Go figure.

Well, I'm certain that your species will find a way to ruin this entire concept. I had a favorite brand of cookie and I wondered just *how* this perfection of delectability could possibly be ruined. But you people came through for me. The company replaced the high-quality chocolate with stuff that was mostly paraffin, and dumped so many preservatives into the recipe that they never were quite crisp.

And some people have no faith in humanity. Pish-tosh! Put your shoulders into it, Mr. and Mrs. Humanity, and I'm absolutely certain that within one generation, podcasts can be worthless and intractable junk of absolutely no value or interest to anybody.

14

Audio Streams

The Skim

You ever get the impression that an organization of otherwise brilliant and creative people just doesn't get it?

(No, I'm not thinking about Lucasfilm and the *Star Wars* prequels. Please, sir, just allow me to continue, all right?)

The iTunes Store and other offerings have allowed the general public to state, loud and clear, that if you charge a reasonable amount of money for recorded content, we're willing to pay it. We will state even *more* clearly that if you're willing to give the content away for free and make it easy to obtain (in the form of a podcast), you'll develop a huge audience and a loyal following.

Y'know? Simple.

And yet, though these really smart people are willing to put their content online, they often do that in such a way that Mr. and Mrs. Digital can't really *use* it.

It's up on their Web site and you can listen to hours of fabulous programming, but you can only access it via an embedded player on the station's Web site. What good is *that*? You're stuck listening to it in front of your computer, instead of enjoying it on your iPhone or iPod Touch while you take your morning four-mile constitutional.

(Oh, all right: my 21-mile drive to buy comic books.)

Well, you shan't be thwarted. There are utilities that can capture whatever audio your PC or Mac is playing, regardless of the source, and immediately encode it into an MP3 file that you can add to your iTunes library. It works with Web sites, it works with media players, it works with satellite radio tuners. Anything.

THE BIG IDEA

The function of these utilities is so basic and fundamental that I need to break it out of that preceding paragraph and let it stand all by itself in its glory:

It can capture any audio playing through your computer to a file that you can import into iTunes and put on an iPhone or iPod Touch.

Well, that's game, set, and match, isn't it? It's a solution to any and all permutations of the question "How do I get this audio onto my device?" Examples:

◘ The BBC streams so much incredibly great content that the sheer awesomeness of it all can affect the tides and confuse migrating birds. But I can only hear this great stuff on a computer with an Internet connection. Plus, they're like five hours ahead of me. I can't be listening to a 9:15 a.m. airing of *The Archers* … that's 4:15 a.m. my time and I'm just getting to bed!

◘ Like … um … well, I think a Biblical reference would work well in this example, but I'm not really all that religious. Wasn't there a dude who went down The Wrong Path before seeing The Light? Let's call him Reggie. Yes, like the Biblical Reggie, you strayed before accepting the wisdom and perfection of Apple and the iPhone. You've bought hundreds of dollars' worth of music from a competing online music service, and they're all locked up with a digital

TIDBIT

As a guy who creates stuff for a living, I ought to acknowledge a question:

Is it *right* to capture audio to a file? Shouldn't we consider the possibility that the creators of a radio show don't podcast their show because they don't *want* people listening on their iPods and iPhones and stuff?

I gotta admit that I don't have an aggressive and arrogant answer to that one. It's certainly wrong to use this software to steal a copy of locked, purchased music that you don't own, for example, but when the audio is on a DVD you bought?

Using an audio-capture utility is almost *righteous*.

Unfortunately, most examples fall in the middle. I suppose it comes down to the advice your parents gave you (if they were good parents, I mean): Would you feel awkward justifying your actions to someone?

I continue to record BBC programming because it's free, and they publish the URLs to their streams openly, and (unlike many radio sites) they don't even use Web ads to subsidize the broadcasts.

But your mileage will vary. Please — I say, sincerely — don't be naughty. One day you're going to wonder why nobody creates any *decent* content any more and the answer is because nobody could make any money doing it.

rights-management system that prevents them from working in any music software other than Windows Media Player. You've seen the error of your ways … *must* you purchase *all* of these tracks all over again in the iTunes Store to get them to play via iTunes?

◘ Okay, go the other way: You like your iPhone, but you also have a swell little Sansa MP3 player made by SanDisk that's dirt-cheap, feather-light, and perfect for your morning run. You've paid hundreds of dollars for iTunes music … why shouldn't you turn those protected iTunes and iPhone-/iPod-only songs into MP3s that you can play on any device?

◘ Through the magic of audio chat, you and four or five people are having an online meeting. You'd like to, you know, *record* all this so that when inevitably the whole project fails and takes the whole company down with it, you can have a swift and conclusive rebuttal to the charge that it was *you* who suggested a buddy-cop movie starring the grown-up cute little kid from *The Sixth Sense* and a wise-cracking cartoon motor scooter voiced by David Spade.

◘ You think that Hunter S. Thompson's stream-of-consciousness rantings in one of the commentary tracks to the *Fear and Loathing in Las Vegas* DVD is just the thing to motivate you through your morning commute. But you're not terribly interested in ripping the movie with one piece of software and then using a *second* piece of software to strip the audio portion into a separate file.

On and on. Audio capture is the sort of tool where you put it on your hard drive …

and then just wait. You can be certain that eventually, it's going to be the solution to *some* sort of problem.

WINDOWS: REPLAY A/V

Applian Technologies' $50 Replay A/V (www.applian.com) is an absolute marvel. It kind of serves to remind me how low my expectations are for apps, after so many years of writing about this stuff. "In a perfect world," I pronounce, as I launch the app for the first time, "if you wanted a piece of software to record *Car Talk* on NPR, you'd search for 'car talk,' the app would find the show automatically, and all the settings would be made for you automatically.

"No, this world is but a vale of tears, and I'm sure that by the time I hear Click and Clack talking about what sort of noise a duck would make if one were trapped inside an air filter, I'll have a PC-shaped hole in my window and a commitment to pursue a new career in agriculture."

But gorblimey. Yes, it really is *that* simple to record a radio show in Replay A/V. You can download a trial copy from www.applian.com or buy a copy there.

Recording a Show by Name (100 Percent Automagically)

Let me do the fancy numbered-lists-and-screenshots thing and formally explain how to record a show:

1. Launch Replay A/V. The main window is shown in Figure 14-1.
2. Click Replay's Media Guide button. This will open a new window containing the Replay Media Guide. It's not incorrect to compare this to the iTunes Store; it's an online entity that helps you search for all manner of online content.

3. Click the Media Guide's Shows button, seen at the top of the Guide window (see Figure 14-2). You'll be taken to a search page.

4. Type the name of the show you'd like to record in the Show Name box, and then click the Find Show button. If the show's listed anywhere in the Guide, you'll see a list of matches (see Figure 14-3). In many cases, the same show will be available from many different online radio stations, airing at different times. Pick your poison.

Figure 14-1

Replay A/V: sticky fingers for PC audio

5. Click the Add button next to the show description you'd like to schedule. Next, you'll see a window where you can tell Replay how you'd like the show to be recorded. Here's the stuff we care about:

   ▶ The Schedule tab lets you set up this show as a recurring recording. By default, Replay will record it every time it airs (the Media Guide database knows that this station airs it every Sunday at 6 p.m.), but this is where you can make it a one-off, for example, or pad the recording by having it start a little early or end a little late.

   ▶ Output is the most important tab in this whole window (see Figure 14-4). Here's where you set up this

recording so that the output always lands directly in the iTunes library, in a format that the iPhone or iPod Touch can handle.

6. Click the Record to this Format pop-up menu and choose Stream Capture as MP3. That's the only iPhone-/iPod-compatible format in the list. Select the Add to iTunes Library checkbox, for obvious reasons, and for good measure, select the Delete Shows Over [X] Days Old checkbox as well. Replay will keep its copy indefinitely unless you check this checkbox (and put in a time limit) or delete the shows manually. You don't need 'em, because they're all going to be copied into iTunes automatically.

7. Click OK.

Better for me to risk stating the obvious than to confuse y'all: Replay A/V can't record any of your scheduled programs unless it's running. It also can't add new recordings to iTunes unless *iTunes* is running as well. So make sure that both apps are launched and ready at all times.

This also means that your *PC* will have to be up and running at the appointed hour. Head on over to Windows's Start menu and choose Start ▶ Control Panel ▶ Performance and Maintenance ▶ Power Options, and set up Windows so that the system never hibernates. You *can* tell Windows to turn off the monitor and the hard drive, though.

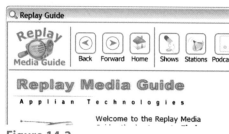

Figure 14-2
The Replay Media Guide's search buttons

Replay will add the show to its to-do list. The rest is elfin' magic. At the right day and time, Replay will contact the streaming-media server that hosts the show and start recording the data "live." You won't hear anything coming out of your PC's speakers but that's okay; it's turning the raw data straight into audio without bothering to clutter your eardrums with it. You can even have other things going on with your PC; if your e-mail client chirps, "You've got mail!" it won't show up in the recording.

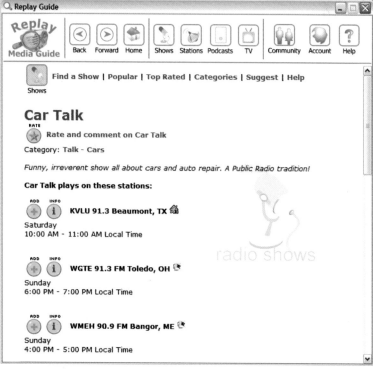

Figure 14-3
Advice about a Miata transmission is now close at hand.

Recording a Show by Radio Station or Server (80 Percent Automagic)

If the Media Guide has never heard of the *SuperMegaHyper Checker Ultra-Ska Nutty Hour* at your local 1,000-watt college radio station, you can still record the show and get Replay to do nearly all the work for you.

1. Open the Media Guide and click the Stations button to search for the station.

2. Enter the station's name or call letters in the Station Name field and click the Find Station button.

3. Click the Add button next to the name of the station you'd like to record. Replay will take you to the same Edit Show window you saw in Figure 14-4. But the information that the Media Guide provided automatically for *Car Talk* will have to be provided manually … by, you know, *you*.

4. In the Basic tab, give the show a name. Go to the Schedule tab and tell Replay what time to start and stop the recording, whether it should just be recorded once on a certain date, or if it should be recorded on a recurring schedule on certain days of the week.

5. Go to the Output tab and use the same iPhone– and iTunes-friendly settings as in the previous example.

6. Click OK to add the new show to the to-do list.

Recording a Show by URL (50 Percent Automagic)

The Replay Media Guide is filled with miracles, have no doubt, but it doesn't know *every-*

thing. It probably doesn't know that the little coffee shop you found in that city you visited on business — the one with the Tuesday night open mic that was absolutely filled with the most breathtakingly bad but vastly entertaining musicians you'd ever heard and that streams the parade of catastrophe and

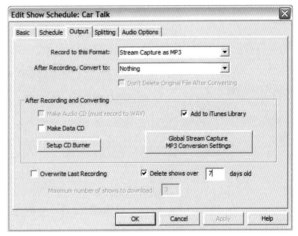

Figure 14-4

Sending the recording straight to iTunes

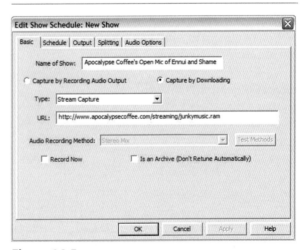

Figure 14-5

Doing it the hard way: adding all the show's details yourself

free-form lute-jazz live every week.

Still, unlike many people, Replay can be taught. All you need is the URL of the audio stream. You can usually find it by visiting the site that promotes or lists the show. Look for a button or a link that says Listen Now or Open in Real Player or some such. Right-click on the link and copy it to the Windows Clipboard.

If you're having no luck locating the elusive URL of that streaming broadcast, Replay can help. Just start the stream playing with Real Player, QuickTime Player, Windows Media Player, or the player that's embedded in your Web browser. Then switch to Replay and click the Stream Capture button.

Replay will sniff around and compile a list of all the URLs that are delivering streaming media to all the software on your PC at that moment. Click the likeliest candidate, click the Add Selection as New Recording button, and Replay will take it from there, acting as though the URL had been delivered from the Media Guide. Then:

1. Click Replay's Manual Add button. You'll be taken straight to Replay's (now-familiar) Edit Show Schedule window (see Figure 14-5).
2. Give the show a name and paste the stream URL in the URL field.
3. Input the settings for Schedule and Output as before.

Recording Whatever's Coming out of Your PC's Speakers Right Now (0 Percent Automagic)

It is yet another testament to Replay's awesomeness that only *now* am I getting to the "Record whatever audio happens to be coming through your PC's speakers" motive that I cited at the top of the chapter. Replay offers so

TIDBIT

Replay is double-plus clever. The Media Guide knows everything it needs to know about every show and every radio station that streams it. And if the station simply leaves the streaming-media file on its servers where any app is free to download it … then Replay will simply download this file in one big blast instead of letting the show slowly stream its way in. Chapter 10 has all the colorful language and pictures explaining how this works.

many features for recording streaming audio that honestly, the only times you'd ever really *need* this feature is if the sound you want to capture isn't coming from the Internet.

Replay A/V is to be commended for not being a total control freak when it comes to this whole recording business. Brian Wilson could have learned a thing from Replay. There, I said it.

Yes, although the app gives you bales of resources for recording shows and streams automatically, it'll also go into Faulknerian Idiot Man-Child mode. Click a button and anything that's playing on your PC will be captured to an audio file:

1. Set up whatever app will be making all that noise — your desktop DVD player software, your audio chat app, Windows Media Player, the Real streaming client — and get it ready so you can start the audio with a minimum of clicking around.
2. In Replay, click the Quick Audio Record button. You'll see the Quick Record

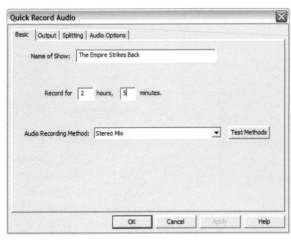

Figure 14-6
Click and record any PC audio in a jiffy

Figure 14-7
Your remote control to Wire-
Tap Pro's features

Audio window (see Figure 14-6).

3. Give the recording a name.

4. In this specific example, I'm recording the audio from my DVD of *The
Empire Strikes Back*. So I'm also telling
Replay to stop recording after 2 hours
and 5 minutes, the running time of the
flick. Plus a little wiggle room.

5. Click the Output tab and make all
those iTunes– and iPhone-ish settings
that we seem to be so keen about.

6. Click OK.

Recording begins immediately and the
Quick Audio Record button turns into a
Stop Recording button. You're ahead of me
on what that does. I can sense it.

MACINTOSH: WIRETAP PRO

Well, I'm just a little bit depressed now,
fellow sensation-seekers. WireTap Pro is a
fine, fine program. I just wish it were more
like Replay A/V, that's all. Ambrosia Software's $20 WireTap Pro (www.ambrosiasw.
com) doesn't offer any of Replay's spectacular

goodities and niceties. It's just a straightforward "capture sound" utility. *Sigh*.

No, no. It's a terrific program. I've just
been spoiled, that's all. Onward, onward.

Recording Whatever's Coming out of Your Mac's Speakers Right Now

WireTap Pro has a very clean, and dare
I say, pretty little controller (see Figure
14-7). Capturing "live" audio to a file (from
a media player like Real Player, the DVD
Player app, iChat, etc.) couldn't be simpler:

1. Click the Record button to start
recording. The LCD-ish numbers at
the bottom of the controller tell you
how long the recording has been running, and how big the file is so far.

2. Click the Stop button to stop. WireTap
Pro will prompt you for a filename and
location.

3. If you fold down the two sealed corners
of a FedEx overnight envelope, you've
got an instant pope hat.

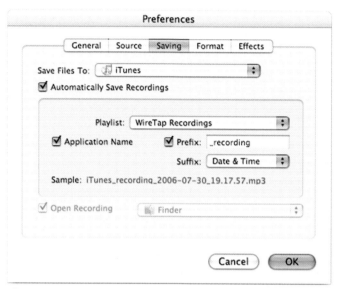

Figure 14-8

Choosing the "where" of WireTap Pro's sound saving

Number 3 has nothing to do with sound recording but the steps for this are so easy that I felt that I needed to beef up the list a little.

Oh, wait! I can complicate things by explaining how to tell WireTap Pro where to save the resulting file, and in what format! Wonderful, wonderful:

1. Choose File ▶ Preferences.
2. Go to the Saving tab of WireTap Pro's Preferences to specify a default destination for the audio (see Figure 14-8).
3. Choose iTunes as the Save Files To destination. All recordings will automatically be sent to your iTunes library. If you check the Automatically Save Recordings option, it'll be saved to iTunes automatically as soon as recording stops. You can also tell WireTap Pro to add the recording to a specific playlist. The only drawback of automatic

saving is that WireTap Pro gives the recording a fairly generic name. Later on, you might not know what the recording is until you give it a listen. WireTap Pro also gives you the option of saving recordings directly to your iPhone or iPod Touch. But that only works if the device happens to be connected to your Mac when the file is finished recording and needs to be saved. Which is a bit of a pain in the butt. Instead, I prefer to save files to a brand-new WireTap Pro Recordings playlist and then set up iTunes to automatically keep this playlist synched to my devices. That way, it'll wind up on my player by hook or by crook.

4. Go to the Format tab to choose a default audio format. Select your favorite format from the list. If you know that you're chiefly going to be recording spoken audio instead of glorious stereophonical music, you can also click the Settings button to choose a configuration that'll result in smaller files. Mono instead of stereo, 22Kbps bit rate instead of 44Kbps, … that sort of thing.
5. Click OK to accept the new settings.

Unlike Replay A/V, when WireTap Pro records everything that comes through your Mac's speakers, it records *everything* that comes through your Mac's speakers. So if your Mail client goes "Bling!" or if there's a "Blort!" signaling that someone would like to start an iChat or if you click into iTunes and start rockin' with some [insert name of a band that you profoundly respect], those noises will turn up on the recording as well.

Recording a Streaming Broadcast

WireTap Pro has quick and clean features for scheduling recordings. It's a pity that you can't just tell it the name of a program and have it fill in the blanks for your automatically, but I suppose I should knock off the Replay references. If I keep going, I'm liable to give WireTap Pro one of those "middle child" syndromes.

Or complexes.

Well, I'll stop, either way.

1. Go to WireTap Pro's Recording Sessions window and click the New but-

ton. You'll see a window with lots of tabs (see Figure 14-9).

2. Give the recording a title (via the Description box). The Saving and Format tabs will be pre-set to the defaults you created in the app's Preferences window.

3. Click the Processing tab to provide WireTap Pro with the URL of the audio stream. Remember, WireTap Pro records all the audio spilling through your Mac. If you leave Real Player (or QuickTime, or the audio stream's live Web page) open, you don't need to provide a URL; at the specified time, WireTap Pro will leap into action and start recording. But it can be pretty dashed annoying to have the local spite-rock station blaring 24 hours just

Figure 14-9
Setting up a new automatic recording

to get the Heavy Metal Traffic Report at 6:50 a.m.. So …

4. Paste the URL for the stream into the first text field of the Processing tab. It contains grayed-out AppleScript, URL, or File text before you replace it. As in the PC example, you can get the URL for the stream by looking for a direct link on the broadcast's Web page … usually it's marked with a Listen or Open in Real Player label or some such.

5. Choose the app that you'll be using to tune in to the stream. By default, Wire-Tap Pro chooses your Safari browser. It's a safe bet because every streaming media player comes with a Safari plug in; it's the one app that's sure to be able to play anything. But for convenience, you'll need WireTap Pro to open the URL in a standalone media player (Real Player or QuickTime Player). That way, you can tell WireTap Pro to Quit the player app when the recording's done. (Why would you want to do that? Because if the URL is the radio station's constant "live" feed, then the URL will remain open even after the recording is complete. So the first recording of the evening will be the 30-minute BBC4 quiz show you wanted. The second recording, made two hours later, will be the NPR report on the woman who makes quilts from used typewriter ribbons … overlaid on top of the audio of whatever's on BBC4 at the moment.)

6. Click Quit or Stop to terminate the sound from the streaming radio station after the recording is complete. Click OK.

The recording info will be saved to Wire-Tap Pro's Recording Sessions list. Whenever

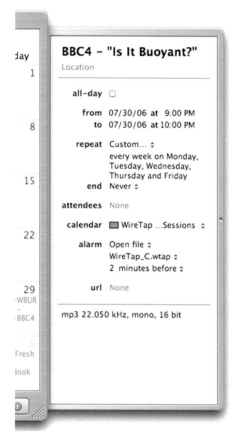

Figure 14-10
Setting up a hot date with the BBC

you select this item in the list and then click the Record Now button, WireTap Pro will record the audio from that URL, starting immediately.

To turn this into a scheduled recording that starts and ends automatically:

1. Select the item and click the Schedule button. WireTap Pro will open the Mac OS's built-in iCal calendar application, and it will create a brand-new appointment for this show (see Figure 14-10). WireTap Pro takes advantage of some of the keen features of iCal and the Mac

OS. WireTap Pro creates its own iCal calendar that contains all its scheduled recordings.

2. Just fill in the date, time and duration details just as you would for any other appointment. When you return to WireTap Pro, you'll find that the particulars have been added to the item in the Sessions list.

And that's it. You just trust things to work, and they do … unless, again, other Mac apps start making noise while WireTap Pro is recording.

RADIOSHIFT FOR MAC: A GREAT LATE ENTRY

Finally, I wish to explain to you once again that life is a vale of tears and that mankind is born unto trouble just as surely as sparks fly upward.

The final, final, *final* deadline for this book — after which this book is locked and no changes are possible —comes in just under 24 hours. I've spent these final few days going through every detail in every chapter, double-checking URLs, prices, making sure that certain products haven't been discontinued, that sort of thing.

"I don't think the price on Rogue Amoeba's Audio Hijack has changed since I wrote that," I thought. "But I ought to check, all the same."

The good news: The price of Audio Hijack Pro is still $32.

The bad news: Yesterday — *yesterday!* — Rogue Amoeba released a new audio app that they'd kept hidden from me until now: Radioshift. Also $32. It's a Mac app that duplicates many, if not most, of the features of Replay A/V that I so lusted after.

Here, check out a screenshot (see Figure 14-11). I've just downloaded and tried it. Sure enough, if you want to record the BBC's *Book at Bedtime*, you just have to say, "Hello, Radioshift? There's this show I really like called *Book at Bedtime*. See what you can do for me." It'll find out when and where it airs and handle all the details for you.

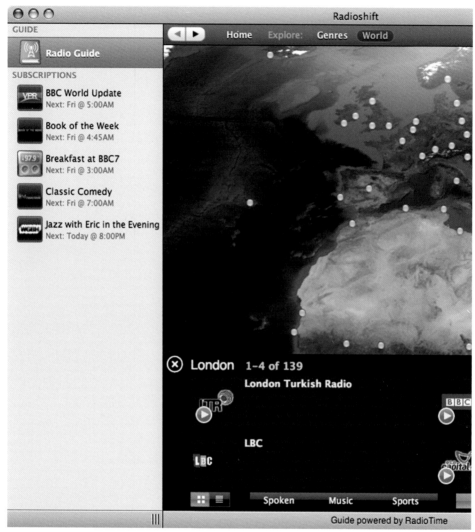

Figure 14-11
Radioshift for Mac: curing Replay A/V envy

It'll even pop up a world map. You can just browse the globe and see what's on the radio in Costa Rica today. Click a button and it's "subscribed." All your subscriptions will be recorded automatically and then you can move them straight into iTunes without any further conversion.

I haven't had time to do much more than download the app and spend an hour pushing buttons and making recordings. But I assure you that the phrase "freaking awesome!" was stated more than once and I urge you to download the free trial and give it a shot.

(That said, I have dispatched an e-mail to Rogue Amoeba explaining the poor timing of this release and informing them that I hate them with the passion of a thousand bleeding suns. The nerve of some people!)

THAT PESKY ETHICAL QUESTION

I think I have an answer for you regarding that little ethical question: Is it okay to record shows streamed from radio stations that apparently don't care to create podcasts?

Absolutely. Because tools like Radioshift and Replay A/V are helping to keep radio alive.

I write a newspaper column, and folks in that biz have been worrying about how they're going to survive in a Webby world. They worry about the future. Well, hogwash: They have a product that folks of all ages on the Web want. The *Chicago Sun-Times* will survive and thrive because it's the reporting and the commentary and the photos that people want. They just don't particularly care to get it on paper as much as they used to.

It's the same deal with radio. It's old-tech, but radio isn't about frequency modulation and cone speakers. It's all about the content. So long as you have programming that people want and so long as there are tools that allow that content to be heard using exciting new methods of delivery, you're immortal.

15

Internet Videos

The Skim

Web Video ■ The World of YouTube ■
Converting Video Files to an iPhone and iPod Touch Format ■
That Pesky "Is It Legal?" Question

Q: What did we ever do before the emergence of YouTube and other Internet video sites?

A: Actual work. We did *actual work.*

Honestly. Like you had to ask. Look at the mighty Boulder Dam, one of the most incredible engineering projects in human history. Beethoven's Ninth Symphony, a tune described as "one of the highest achievements of man," so powerful that it served as the hopeful anthem to the closure of an international conflict that claimed tens of millions of lives. Or the Great Pyramid at Giza, whose monumental form and seething mysteries have endured through five millennia.

Ask yourself: "Do you think the people who accomplished these great deeds spent *any* amount of time watching some guy from Encino attempt to play *The Simpsons* theme on a calliope made of soda bottles and Mentos?"

Yes, I'm just as depressed as you are. But strength comes from knowledge.

Welp, we're stuck with this sad state of affairs. The good news is that the utter collapse of all civilization, though inevitable, won't really start becoming a nuisance until our as-yet-unborn grandchildren turn 40. So for now, we can download some of the better videos and enjoy them on our iPhone and iPod Touch.

WEB VIDEO

The process boils down to this:

1. Pull the video down off the Web and into a video file on your computer.
2. Convert that file into a format that your iPhone can play.

In the olden days — and sadly, I'm talking about 2004 and parts of 2005, here — finding video was a tough process, and figuring out where and how to download it was something of a black art. You had to examine the Web page's raw HTML and try to figure out where the actual video file was stored and then bamboozle the Web server into allowing you to download it directly instead of just passively playing it through the Web browser.

Nowadays, the situation has been streamlined. Either the video's owners are absolutely *delighted* to download and enjoy the file (so much so that they've put a big, juicy Download for iPod/iPhone button on the Web page) or they've locked it up so well that it's really not likely that whatever-it-is is going to be worth the effort.

How to illustrate this phenomenon? I suppose the most popular example is Google Video, which often contains an embedded Download button.

But just last week, the new trailer for *Iron Man* was released and it looks so damned awesome that these four minutes alone have finally erased the horrors I suffered from all the *Batman* movies that were directed by Joel Schumacher. I think you'll agree that Figure 15-1 looks a lot cooler than any boring old Google Video page.

Oh how I envy you, Reader of the Future,

who might be reading this after 05/02/08 and are in a position to know just exactly how awesome this movie is. Until then, I and the other readers have only www.apple.com/trailers to tide us over.

Some sites (like Apple's own movie trailer page, naturally) will download the video and add it to your iTunes library in one step.

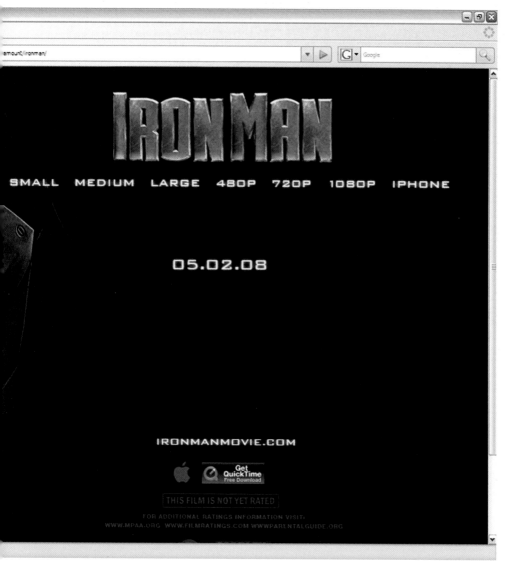

Figure 15-1
A completely gratuitous *Iron Man* screenshot, ostensibly to show you a Download for iPhone button

Otherwise, you'll wind up with an MP4 video file in your browser's download folder. Drag it into iTunes and you can synch it to your iPhone or iPod Touch.

THE WORLD OF YOUTUBE

But when we're talking about Internet video here in the Push-Button World of the Future, we're talking about YouTube and

157

its various clones. These sites actually have plenty of great content and lots of videos of someone's ferret wobbling around the floor wearing a lime rind as a helmet — but you take the good with the bad. Playing the video within the service's browser is a piece of cake, but getting at that rich, nougaty center of iPhone-able data takes a bit of work.

In fact, there's so much interest in this sort of function that there are lots of third-party utilities you can buy that offer you point-and-shoot downloading and conversions. But they usually have two problems:

- They tend to be overpriced. They range from fifteen bucks to fifty and they all do the exact same thing. Usually (like DVD-ripping utilities) they're actually based on a piece of software that some other programmer designed and gave away for the good of all users everywhere. Weasels shouldn't profit.

- But more than that… they don't work for very long. Even the ones that can *only* handle YouTube videos tend to quit working all of a sudden, days or months

after you buy it. These apps interact with YouTube in ways that the service never really intended, so when the service makes a small change to the way it organizes and presents its data, suddenly the app's little trick no longer works and you have to just hope that a new version is released.

So I'm telling you upfront that the procedures I'm giving you *aren't* the simplest and the most streamlined way of going about this. But they *are* the most foolproof, and they're free, free, free.

Our main weapon here is not a desktop app but a Web site: www.keepvid.com (see Figure 15-2). It's brilliant. All the special mojo for locating and retrieving the video file you want is located on KeepVid's servers, so whenever YouTube makes a change that "breaks" the old mojo, KeepVid's developers invisibly update their tool so that it continues to work.

It also supports a *monster* list of video sites. The commercial apps are lucky to support YouTube and one or two others. But

TIP

Lately, I've been trying out a Web service called Vixy (www.vixy.net) for downloading and converting iPhone– and iPod Touch-compatible YouTube videos. It's a two-step process and no software is required … plus it's free. It's all done through a single Web page.

It's really interesting. It works a lot like KeepVid: Copy the URL to the embedded video, paste it into Vixy's online form, and click a button. Vixy will locate the source file, convert it to an iPhone-/iPod-compatible format, and then give you a link so you can download it to your desktop.

You know what? It works.

Awesome. But it's also rather new, and I honestly have no idea how long it'll be around. I don't even know if a week after this book hits the shelves, this nice little Web page will be loaded with ads for porn sites.

Still, it's too good not to mention. And heck, lots of people like porn sites. Who am I to judge?

Figure 15-2
KeepVid.com, your universal video grabber

KeepVid will work with dang-near every sharing site out there.

And though it's not a one-click operation, downloading the video is still extremely piece-of-cake-like in form and function. You give KeepVid the URL of the video and it'll generate a link from which you can download the video. So:

1. Copy the URL of the video. And here I don't mean the YouTube URL from your browser's address bar. No, I mean that you should hunt for what the Web site calls a "permalink," which is a link to this content that doesn't change from user to user. You can see an example of a permalink in Figure 15-3.

2. Go to www.keepvid.com.

TIDBIT

YouTube's partnership with Apple has led to the video site's decision to convert much of its content to an inherently iPhone-/iPod Touch-friendly format, MPEG-4 (a.k.a. MP4). So if KeepVid finds a file that ends in .mp4 — the filename extension for MPEG-4 files — it's likely that the file can go into iTunes and thence your iPhone or iPod Touch without any further work necessary. Fingers crossed on that one.

Figure 15-3
A permalink to a video on YouTube.com

Figure 15-4
Success! KeepVid has located the actual video file on YouTube's servers.

3. Paste the URL into KeepVid's Download field.

4. Click Download. Don't worry about the pop-up menu to the right of the link box; KeepVid will automatically figure out what service the video is on, and will select the correct technique to figure out the URL. KeepVid will then generate a Download Link to the video file (see Figure 15-4).

5. Right-click or Control+click on this link and choose Save to start downloading the file to your computer.

KeepVid might tell you to rename the file so that the name ends in .flv. Most of the content on Google Video and YouTube arrives in the Flash Video format (that's what the .flv filename extension means). KeepVid has no way of knowing what to call this file, so you're free to name it something sensible, such as "AwesomeRollerbladeWipeout-WhereTheDudeTotallyGetsHitInTheGroin-LikeAMillionTimes.flv."

Cool. Now you have a video that *used* to be on YouTube (or some other site) and now it's on your desktop. In a format that iPhone and iPod can't understand. Alas, mankind is born unto trouble as surely as sparks fly upward. But stick with it, because you're not done yet.

CONVERTING VIDEO FILES TO AN IPHONE AND IPOD TOUCH FORMAT

So now you've downloaded a video file that won't work on your iPhone. Well, slugger, I know that you're feeling kind of blue right now, but you need to realize that life is full of disappointments. It's not our problems that define us, … it's how we *overcome* those problems.

Sorry. I have no kids and my innate parenting and nurturing skills sometimes need to find an outlet.

You just need to process those video files with a conversion utility … and while it's a crowded market, there are two great ones for PCs and Macs that are free for the downloading.

Windows: Videora's iPod Converter

I'll tell you the honest truth: There isn't one clear "top of the class" video conversion utility for Windows. I'll quickly run down the finalists, though:

▪ Total Video Converter from iTinySoft (www.itinysoft.com) is hands-down the fastest and most full-featured video transcoder utility out there. No matter

Figure 15-5
Videora's iPod Converter transmogrifies Flash video into iPhone and iPod Touch video.

what sort of video file you have or what you want to do with it, TVC can handle the job. It *should* be declared the winner ... but it costs close to fifty bucks. That's not a lot of money, but there are a whole bunch of utilities that aren't nearly so ambitious but that do get the job done and do it for free. Apps like ...

◘ MediaCoder is a free open-source app (meaning, written by a charitable programmer for the good of the community), which you can download from

http://mediacoder.sourceforge.net. It's the standard-bearer for everything that's good and not-so-good about open-source software. It's intensely powerful (easily the match of TVC) and nearly impossible to use unless the primary mineral in your blood is copper, like Mr. Spock.

◘ But let's also mention Replay Converter from Applian Technologies (www.applian.com), which has a nice, simple one-(small)-window interface. Also, Applian are the generous folks behind that free KeepVid tool. But the app costs thirty bucks, and here it is three months after the iPhone has been released and they still haven't updated it to support that larger screen. Okay, true, a typical YouTube video isn't as big as that anyway. But still.

But they're all winners just for showing up and participating in live theater. Let's give them all a great big hand. No, no, let's *really* let 'em hear it!

Spiffy. So the Windows app I'm finally recommending to you is Videora iPod Converter. It's a free download from www.videora.com.

Figure 15-5 shows the main conversion window. It ain't the prettiest thing you've ever seen, but the results are swell and you can't argue with the price. Figure 15-5 shows Videora in its so-called "power mode," which oddly enough is simpler than the so-called "normal mode."

Even when you're going for Power, the procedure is attractively linear. All the necessary settings are at the bottom of the window and you just move from top to bottom:

1. Click the Select File button and select the .flv file you want converted.

2. Click the Browse button on the next line and choose a location for the converted video file. Or accept the default location, a Converted Videos folder that the app will create for you inside your Documents folder.

3. Click in the Title box and give the converted video a name that humans like yourself (presumably) can understand.

4. Choose iPhone or iPod, as appropriate, from the Device pop-up menu.

5. Admire the Profile pop-up menu but *do not* touch it. Videora has chosen the correct settings (format, picture size, image quality) for you.

6. Click Start Converting.

Annnnnnd wait. Transcoding a Flash video file into an iPhone-/iPod Touch-compatible MP4 file can easily take twice as long as the running time of the original video. I believe that the talking School Days Barbie doll said it best when she opined, "Math is *hard!*"

Eventually the toast will indeed pop up, and you can toss the resulting video file right into your iTunes library without any further ado.

Macintosh: iSquint

Hello, hello: This is more like it. iSquint is precisely the sort of app you're hoping to find (see Figure 15-6). It's a transcoder that's so good, there's really no need to mention any other. Go to www.isquint.org and download the freebie. It makes the whole process simple and efficient:

1. Add files to iSquint's conversion queue. You can either drag the files right into the list or you can bring up the standard Mac file picker by clicking the little plus (+) button.

2. Select a size. iSquint can convert movies to either the smaller iPod size, or a larger size suitable for TV viewing. As right-thinking iPhone and iPod Touch owners, we have nice big screens, so go ahead and choose TV.

3. Select the Add to iTunes checkbox to have iSquint add the resulting video files to your iTunes library as soon as they're finished.

4. Go down to the Saving In box and click the Change button to select a location for the converted files.

5. Click Start to get the ball rolling.

And as usual, this is an excellent time to

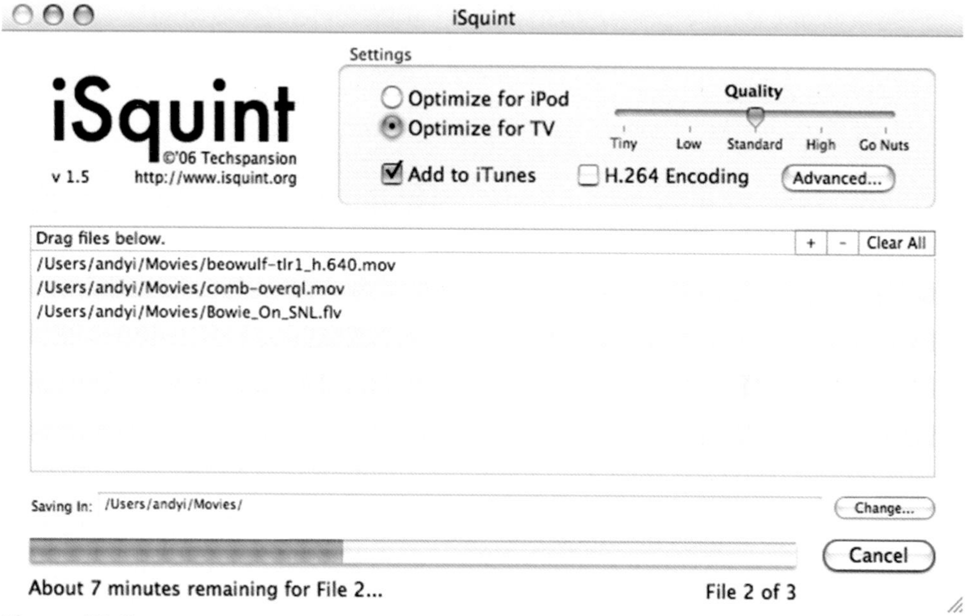

Figure 15-6
iSquint: one Mac transcoder to unite them all

get to know your spouse and children a little better. Because this conversion is going to take a while and yes, you'll be *that* bored.

Oh, one thing I skipped: There is indeed a Quality control but it's generally not worth messing around with. You're starting off with a video file that was sized and compressed for YouTube so increasing that control won't really make the video look any better.

Technically you'll get better video if you click the H.264 Encoding option. But the increase in quality isn't dramatic and the increase in conversion time is devastating. Check it, and you have enough time to actually take the family out to a session of kite flying followed by a picnic lunch. Leave it unchecked and you're back at your computer before you've finished one game of Sorry all the way through.

THAT PESKY 'IS IT LEGAL?' QUESTION

It's just a *little* bit itchy to reflect upon the fact that most of the really good content on YouTube, Google Video, iFilm, et al. is up there illegally. But it's mostly because it's stuff that nobody cares to sell. Pilot episodes of brilliant TV shows that never made it into a series. Talk-show appearances by long-dead celebs. Movies whose ownership is tied up under so many layers of production companies and communications internationals and ex-spouses and live-in lovers that they'd never ever see the light of day if not for the fact that someone had an old VHS copy and decided to put it up on YouTube.

So sure, I make fun of the video of the semipro skateboarder who *thought* he'd be teaching hundreds of fans how to do a 720

Sherman Helmsley with a half-weezie layback, but who instead wound up teaching hundreds of thousands of office workers that a steady job with good health insurance is nothing to scoff at. He also showed hundreds of med students how it's possible for someone to wind up with a parking meter wedged significantly within a very naughty place.

Why? Because, dude, … he *totally* wiped out. It was awesome.

Nonetheless, so long as great stuff is out there that's not for sale elsewhere, video sites are always worth a browse. Earlier today, I downloaded a documentary about legendary comic-book artist Steve Ditko that aired two days ago on the BBC. Fat chance of any channel over *here* picking that up. It's now on my iPhone and I shall enjoy it guilt-free when I board a plane in a couple of days.

16

How to Download Free Music and Get Away with It

The Skim

The Case for Going Legal ■ Becoming a Pawn in a Marketing Plan ■
Helping Preserve Our Cultural Heritage ■
Finding Free Music

Here's why you shouldn't download music illegally:
   Er …
   Hang on. It's coming.
   Okay, well, I just want to sort of appeal to your higher nature, here. I realize that taking up the cause of the music industry in the piracy issue is a lot like watching *It's a Wonderful Life* and wondering why that awful Harry Bailey doesn't just hand over the Building & Loan to Mr. Potter so that this sweet old man can live out his dream of turning a dull little town into a nigh-lawless zone of sin, corruption, and a nightmarish arena for the steady wearing-down of human souls. Have you never *been* to Las Vegas? One pass through the $2.49 breakfast buffet at the Riviera and you'll realize that the unregulated free-market system works just fine and Potter had the right idea.
   Nonetheless, I should point out that downloading MP3 files of copy-righted music illegally from Those Kinds Of Places is simply wrong. And if that's not good enough reason, I should explain that the network

technologies that power Those Kinds Of Places were by no means designed to keep their users' identities secret. With far less money to count, the recording industry has more time to spend on terrifying vendettas.

So if you *do* insist on stealing music, I suggest you make it The Who's *Quadrophenia* or perhaps Elvis Costello's *My Aim Is True.* Because as bad as it is to go through months of legal proceedings followed by thousands of dollars in fines and perhaps even a few months of jail time, it's going to feel a lot worse if you brought all this down on your head for a copy of *American Idol: Greatest Moments Season 4.*

Better to just tread the straight and narrow path, I say. Particularly when there are so many ways of getting free music the legal way.

THE CASE FOR GOING LEGAL

Many people ridicule the recording industry's copyright watchdogs, and for good reason: Their excesses are, well, so *excessive.* You could praise them for their unusual dedication and determination even when it's been demonstrably proven that the person they're prosecuting into bankruptcy is an octogenarian retiree who doesn't even own a computer.

You might even believe that they're a separate branch of the evolutionary tree, with seven webbed toes on each foot. But that wouldn't change the fact that piracy is wrong. You want it? You gotta pay for it. Period.

But if the moral angle doesn't work for you, keep in mind that it's a fairly automated process to detect illegal music downloads. The recording industry's copyright goons are aware of that illegal file-sharing site well before you. Also be aware that even though

Figure 16-1

Beats for deadbeats: free music and video from the iTunes Store

you never provided a name and address, your computer left a sequence of digits that can trace the download all the way back to your house, and that the aforementioned goons, with one e-mail to your Internet service provider, can exchange these digits for a name and address.

So it's wrong and it's dangerous.

And most music sucks, anyway. Do you really want a $3,000 fine for a song from a band that, 20 years from now, you'll swear to your kids that you never liked or listened to?

BECOMING A PAWN IN A MARKETING PLAN

Yes indeed, it's possible to (a) download music, (b) download copyrighted music by name-brand artists, (c) not pay a dime for it, and most bizarre of all, (d) play right into the hands of the recording industry.

It's all merchandising, promotion, and the desire to "go viral." Record companies regularly seed the major commercial music stores with tracks that you can download for free. Let me point you to the most reliable ones.

iTunes Music Store

Naturally, the iTunes Store is your first and simplest click. The store's front door always

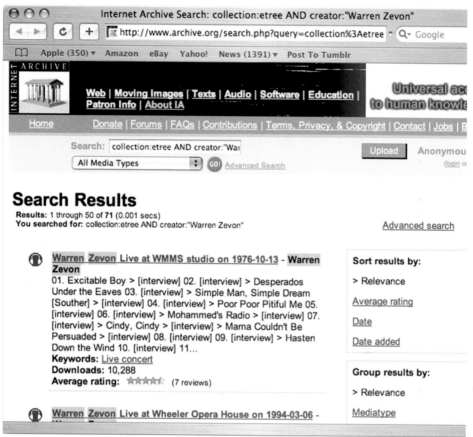

Figure 16-2
Internet Archive: free music with a higher calling

contains a few links to free downloads. Going to www.apple.com/itunes/freesingle will always show you the spotlighted free single of the week. But there are usually others, too. You'll find these links in a special box at the entrance to the store (see Figure 16-1).

Naturally, you won't exactly be spending hours poring through the free selections; usually there are only a handful of freebies available at any given time, and they're only available for a limited time.

But iTunes shoppers are such a huge and

important part of the music market that music publishers are often willing to give away tracks by chart-topping acts instead of the factory-floor sweepings you'd expect to see. I mean, seriously: Paul McCartney? Bruce Springsteen? These people aren't exactly unsigned acts playing at the Bitter Dregs Coffeehouse in Nortonville, Rhode Island.

You do indeed have to look for these freebies, but if you're not interested in scouring the store yourself, you can bookmark the

Showing results 1 - 10 out of **13993** for *yonder mountain string band*

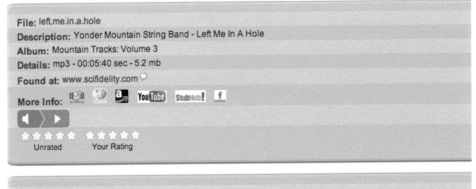

Figure 16-3
Skreemr: like a big rabid bat that gets tangled in your hair and drops music all over you

Free iTunes Store Downloads blog (www. itsfreedownloads.com). This regularly updated blog maintains a list of not just the free music downloads but also free audio-books and videos. Best of all, you can sub-scribe to its RSS feed in your Web browser or newsreader, and automatically be notified of new freebies.

AOL Music

AOL, following the iTunes model, hides its freebies at the bottom of the page (at http://music.aol.com). AOL is hoping that you'll sign up for its subscription music ser-vice. The selections usually aren't as sweet as what you'll find on iTunes, but AOL is worth

a regular peek because it often snags some real gems.

HELPING PRESERVE OUR CULTURAL HERITAGE

Or at least that's how you feel when you visit the Internet Archive (www.archive.org). The Internet Archive, a nonprofit member of the American Library Association, is no mere repository of audio files. It has taken on a goal of protecting and preserving content and making it available to current and future generations.

It's an ambitious project. The Internet Archive will show you Web pages stretch-ing back to the very start of the World Wide

Web. Classic books and essays are available as electronic texts. Movies, television shows, old software, and, yes, music — all from artists who support the Internet Archive's cause (see Figure 16-2).

If you think this audio archive contains public-domain jug-band music transferred off wax Edison cylinders, you would be correct.

But it also contains modern tunes, speeches, conferences, and the largest and best-indexed collection of legal concert recordings available anywhere many from major, currently touring groups. With tens of thousands of music files available, it's easy to fill an iPhone to the brim from the Internet Archive alone.

FINDING FREE MUSIC

The sites I've mentioned aren't the only spots where you can find free music. Practically 99 percent of the others fall into a few predictable categories:

- Free music, but you can't actually download it. It's like a radio station where you can be your own deejay. Which is fine if you're trying to kill some time at work, but not so good if you want to fill an iPhone.
- Free music, but chiefly it's a way to sneak spyware, adware, keystroke loggers, and other nasty maliciousness onto your system. Which is why you need to be careful about Googling for "free music downloads." It's there with "free ringtones," "free wallpaper," and "Do you share a credit-card or Social Security number with a famous celebrity? Take our free online quiz and find out!" — it's something of a red-flag phrase for *fraud.*
- Free, downloadable music, no fooling, but it's just a few specific bands. Which

is terrific from my point of view as I have hundreds of pages to fill, but what help is that to you, the consumer?

No, instead I'll press on and talk about ways to locate free music through search engines.

Music-Specific Search Engines

There's so much free and legal music out there that search engines have arrive specifically to help you find the stuff. Skreemr (www.skreemr.com) is one of the broadest, allowing you to perform a search based on genre, band name, performers, even the bit rate and duration of the tracks (see Figure 16-3).

Generic search engines such as Yahoo Search also allow you to limit your focus to just music files. But the kudos-of-kudos go to www.dogpile.com (see Figure 16-4). Not only does it have a specific music-search feature but (now get this) it's a search engine that searches *search engines.* So doing a single Dogpile search for "Yonder Mountain" (awesome bluegrass band, incidentally) is nearly

TROUBLE

The Web is also obviously a powerful tool for a band that wants to delude itself and its belief in the ability of a Kiss-influenced Christopher Cross tribute band to make it in the industry. All I'm saying is that just because your band's site got more than 210 visitors last month it doesn't mean it's time to tell your boss at the shoe warehouse where he can go.

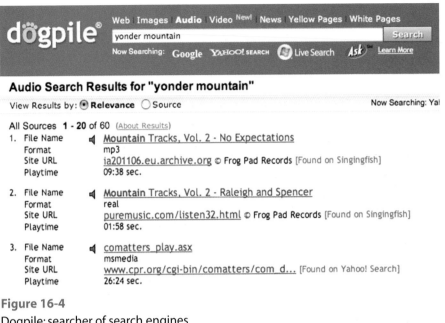

Figure 16-4
Dogpile: searcher of search engines

as good as doing a half-dozen searches on all the other search sites.

Not all the links returned by Dogpile will be to downloadable MP3 files, but it clearly lists the format of the music track. So it's easy to target just those links that you can load on your iPhone and enjoy on a motorcycle.

Freebies from Music Blogs

The Web is obviously a powerful tool for a band that wants to promote itself and its music.

And thousands of lower-tier bands offer their MP3s on their personal sites as an enticement to maybe drive 30 miles to a hole-in-the-wall venue just outside of Pittsburgh and pay a $5 cover charge to see 'em play live. But how to *find* these sites?

Well, you can try a straight-up Google search for the sort of music you like ("blue-

grass MP3 download") and keep clicking until you get lucky. Or, you could subscribe to any of a number of music-oriented blogs. Good luck; when I did, there were exactly 13,218 of them.

Or, you could visit *one* blog that keeps tabs on all the music being linked from all the *other* music blogs. The Hype Machine (www.hypem.com) is a blog in which every item is simply a link to a track that's recently become available through another music blog or podcast (see Figure 16-5).

Results can be a bit scattershot; it gives you the firehose treatment, as opposed to a nice friendly clickable button marked "Music you'd be likely to show half an interest in." But the side benefit is that it doesn't take long before you've bookmarked a bunch of music sites that regularly feature the music that the parents of today and the kids of

THE HYPE MACHINE

about   radio +

Find music you never knew you liked

Listen to search results

Pop-up Flash Player

or listen in your media player   (What's this?)

What's hot

Most Blogged
Rilo Kiley
Radiohead
The New Pornographers
M.I.A.
Josh Ritter
view more >>

Popular Sear
Radio No
Madonna 1
Mia
Rilo Kiley
Bruce Sprin

Results for: bluegrass

eMusic has at least **409** mp3 tracks like this. _check them out_

Jun 15	**The Avett Brothers - Bluegrass, Die Die Die** _amazon_ _itunes_ posted by Radio Free Chicago in "The Avett Brothers @ House o..." _read »_
Jun 15	**The Legendary Shack Sha... - Blood on the Bluegrass** _amazon_ _itunes_ posted by ninebullets.net in "Tampa/St. Pete...To Do&#..." _read »_
Jun 12	**The Avett Brothers - Bluegrass, Paranoia In Bb Major** _amazon_ _itunes_ posted by ThaBombShelter in "Bluegrass Battle Royale Cage..." _read »_
Jun 12	**David Lee Roth with the... - Jump**

Figure 16-5
Hype Machine: all the music in the blogosphere, at a glance

tomorrow can't abide.

I also really dig Hype Machine's Popular button: One click takes you to all the music that the other humans seems to be enjoying at the moment. It's a great vector for discovering new bands and genres.

Googling for Tunes

Eventually, it comes down to rummaging through dumpsters and trash cans for scraps of entertainment.

At least that's what it _feels_ like when you start using Google to locate music files. It's a

hopelessly random tool for this sort of thing. It works a treat if you click the search box armed with the name of a fantastic band that you heard playing in Harvard Square, but when you plug the phrase "music I'm not already sick and tired of" into the search box Google doesn't return the results that it ought to.

Google _could_ become a monster tool for finding and downloading free music. But as of this writing, it doesn't appear to be interested in giving us that sort of tool. Google does have a Music Search feature, but all it

means is that if you search for Janis Joplin, it'll begin its list of search results with a list of albums, and music services where you can purchase them.

The next best thing is to exploit one of Google's advanced search features. I'll cut to the chase and give you a sample Google search string:

```
bluegrass intitle:index.of +"last modified" +"parent
directory" +mp3 +"" –htm –html –php –asp
```

Yes, I know. Breathe in. Breathe out. It's all going to be okay.

If you're absolutely terrified of what you've just seen, then you simply replace "bluegrass" with any word or words that describe the sort of music you want to find. Hold your nose and type the rest of the string as is. You don't have to know what it means.

If you're *not* dealing with an adrenaline-fueled "flight response" right now, then sit back while I explain what's going on.

We're telling Google that we *don't* want to search for conventional Web pages. We want Google to find *directory* pages. When someone publishes an open folder of files on their Web server — either to explicitly allow strangers to connect to that folder and copy files, or just as a central repository for all the images, music, etc. that the Web site's visi-tors can download by clicking a link — the Web server displays those files in a standard formatted list entitled "Index of…" with column headers that read "last modified" and "parent directory" and the like.

So this search string instructs Google to please find any MP3 files in any open direc-tories that contain the word "bluegrass" but that are *not* HTML files or PHP scripts or any other little files that represent actual Web pages.

Plug this into Google and it's all over but

Listen to search results

Pop-up Flash Player

or listen in your media player   (What's this?)

What's hot

Most Blogged
Rilo Kiley
Radiohead
The New Pornographers
M.I.A.
Josh Ritter
view more >>

Popular Sear
Radio No
Madonna 1
Mia
Rilo Kiley
Bruce Sprinc

Results for: bluegrass

eMusic has at least **409** mp3 tracks like this. *check them out*

Jun 15   **The Avett Brothers - Bluegrass, Die Die Die** *amazon* *itunes*
posted by Radio Free Chicago in "The Avett Brothers @ House o..." *read »*

Jun 15   **The Legendary Shack Sha... - Blood on the Bluegrass** *amazon* *itunes*
posted by ninebullets.net in "Tampa/St. Pete...To Do&#..." *read »*

Jun 12   **The Avett Brothers - Bluegrass, Paranoia In Bb Major** *amazon* *itunes*
posted by ThaBombShelter in "Bluegrass Battle Royale Cage..." *read »*

Jun 12   **David Lee Roth with the... - Jump**

Figure 16-6
Del.icio.us MP3 bookmarks: like *American Idol* voting, only you're certain that everyone who "voted" is smart enough to know how to operate a computer

the endless wading through dozens and dozens of pages of results.

Delicious Music

There's a similar trick that uses Del.icio.us, the (hypermegasuperawesome) community-based Web directory. Del.icio.us — yes, that's a URL: del.icio.us — is a valuable tool for navigating the Web. Its users can "publish" bookmarks to the Del.icio.us Web site, tagged with keywords that make it easy to find pages that fit certain categories.

Search Google for "poker tips" and it will return every Web page everywhere that contains those two words.

But if you search Del.icio.us with those words, it only returns Web pages that Del.icio.us's users have personally tagged with those two descriptive words, and (hooray!) were considered valuable enough to actually bookmark. So nearly every page it returns is pure Tabasco.

You can indeed search for "free music" and get lots of productive hits. But Del.

Figure 16-7
SeeqPod is like having 1,000 terabytes of music on your iPhone or iPod Touch at all times.

icio.us (unlike Google) will search specifically for music files if you know how to ask. Bookmark this URL: http://del.icio.us/tag/system:filetype:mp3. The result is a list of recently bookmarked MP3 files that Del.icio.us's users have located and saved all over the Web (see Figure 16-6).

You can also try http://del.icio.us/popular/system:filetype:mp3 to just check out the MP3s that lots and lots of Del.icio.us users have deemed popular.

SeeqPod

I won't name any names, but there are so many bitterly fought battles in the world today in which it's pretty clear that the reasons for the fight have become secondary to the fight itself. A technology or some sort

of solution comes along and it's bleedingly obvious that here, we can make *everybody* happy.

This is what struck me when I first tried SeeqPod (www.seeqpod.com). This free service finds music on the Net. Some of it's free and legal, some isn't. But the big deal is that this Web site *doesn't allow you to download anything*. You search for music and SeeqPod obligingly locates the file online and plays it for you in an online player.

SeeqPod is of particular interest to us because it has a *terrific* iPhone app. Point your iPhone's browser to www.seeqpod.com/iphone and feast your eyes (see Figure 16-7).

Tap on any song or any of SeeqPod's user-generated playlists and the music will start streaming in right from your Internet connection. It's just music, so you don't even necessarily need to have a working Wi-Fi connection. You can be walking along the street and suddenly indulge a whim to hear a Buckwheat Zydeco album that's nowhere on your iPhone and six or seven taps later, hey, cool, you're walking down the street and listening to a Buckwheat Zydeco album.

There are two potential misconceptions that I want to dispel before we move on. First, when I say that downloading music illegally is just plain wrong, I'm not winking furiously as I do so. The recording industry is guilty of a great many sins, but that doesn't make piracy right. Just don't do it.

I'd also like to state that just because I happened to use bluegrass music for most of my search examples it doesn't mean that I'm, you know, not all hip and stuff. Remember when I mentioned plugging "sick and tired of" into Google and getting one of my favorite albums? That album is *Suicidal Tendencies*, not a cast album from *The Lawrence Welk Show*.

PART IV

The Office

17

Calendars and Contacts

The Skim

Hmm. So I suppose I can't talk you out of this idea. No matter what I say, you're going to use your iPhone or your iPod Touch to store an address book and a personal calendar.

No, I can't say that I recommend it. Both increase the risk of human social contact and that sort of thing can really cut into the time you have available to translate *The Wizard of Oz* into Klingon.

If you're using Microsoft Outlook or the standard Mac OS apps (iCal and Address Book) to manage your calendars and contacts on the desktop, you have this bit covered already. iTunes automagically synchs your data to the device.

If you're *not,* you can still synch your personal life. You'll just have to slosh your contacts and appointments around a little bit first.

NONSTANDARD CALENDAR AND CONTACT APPS

So for some unfathomable reason you're not free to use Outlook or the standard Mac apps for managing your calendars and contacts. I'm guessing it has something to do with an arbitrary rule that someone at your company put into place after realizing that they've been promoted way above their personal skill set and desperately needed to do *something* to signify that they have actual power and authority. Let's say your company has standardized on DiscoAppointmentsAndFolks 3.0.

To get all that data into your iPhone or iPod Touch you have to use one of iTunes's approved apps as a go-between. That is, instead of iTunes automatically synching all your data every time you plug your device into your desktop, you first manually export all your DiscoAppointmentsAndFolks data to Outlook, or iCal and Address Book. *Then* you plug in your iPhone.

See? iTunes is still working with the familiar apps it knows and loves.

You do this via the international standards of love for moving this sort of data between two different apps:

- ☑ vCard format is used for address book data.
- ☑ iCalendar format is used for calendar data. And just to make sure there's as much confusion as can possibly be, it's sometimes shortened to "iCal." During explanations like these, it's inevitably lengthened to "iCal, not to be confused with the calendar app that ships on all Macs."

Most modern apps can export their data in both of these formats.

EXPORTING AND IMPORTING DATA TO MAKE IT SYNCH!

Importing the data into the Mac OS is alluringly cakelike. iCal has an easy-as-pie Import command. Just point it at the exported data and you're in business. Ditto for the Address Book. Choose File ▶ Import ▶ vCards and then navigate to the file that contains all your exported contacts.

On the Windows side, things are just a *bit* trickier. And here I'm using "a bit trickier" to act as an efficient substitute for about two

pages worth of passionate screeding about why the devil an important, industry-leading app like Microsoft Outlook doesn't directly support the most popular contact data interchange format on the whole bloody planet.

iCalendar data imports just fine into Outlook. But what's up with the vCard support? It can import vCard data, but (oh, dear God) *only the first name in the file.* If you have 500 names in there, it'll stop with "AAAAAA Custom Paint and Body, Inc.," ignoring all the rest.

So unless you're a way more patient person than I am, go to http://vsync.4team.biz and buy the vSync plug-in for Outlook. It integrates into the app seamlessly, adding its own Import and Export buttons to the user interface, and adds *actual* support for vCard, instead of this purely ceremonial feature that Microsoft slapped in there. And it's quite reasonably priced at about $15.

It's wonderful that even the simplest, most straightforward, and most reliable feature on this whole phone has at least one or two gotchas, isn't it?

I speak of course from the point of view of somebody who makes his living writing about technology. Honestly, if all this stuff worked the way it ought to, I'd probably be loading trucks at the UPS depot for a living.

Come to think of it, if I worked at UPS I'd probably be on a group dental plan instead of having to sell my collectible porcelain figurines every time I need a cavity filled.

Damn. I just brought myself down without even planning it…

18

Clippings and Trivial Ephemera

The Skim

"I write doo-dads, because it's a doo-dad sort of town." Thus wrote Dorothy Parker, the genius columnist, poet, and wit.

I suppose just for the sake of balance and accuracy I should also include an additional Parker quote: "*BATS! Giant, hairy bats! Circling my typewriter and pelting me with copper spoons filled with jam! AIEEEE!!!*"

She was a treasure of American literature but the poor girl did drink an *awful* lot, you know.

Nonetheless, she had a solid point about doo-dads. If anything, the communal town in which we all live is even doo-daddier today than it was in Parker's time. Your life is filled with little bits of information that defy any ready organization or catchall filing system. Still, you need 'em. What's the address of that luncheonette on Lexington Avenue you wanted to visit on your way to the Metropolitan Museum of Art? What are the museum's hours? What bus do you need to take to get from the museum to your friend's place in SoHo afterward?

One afternoon in New York City, three absolutely essential doo-dads. And this was just for a *fun* afternoon. When there's business and meet-

ings and money involved, you can accumulate dozens of these things over the course of a week.

WHY NOT NOTEPAD?

Now then. If you've spent any time playing with your iPhone, the phrase "tons of pieces of seemingly random and unconnected information with barely any sense or order" conjures up one thought: Notepad.

("Also, 'This very book,'" says my girlfriend, reading over my shoulder as I type. I include this comment so that on future first dates with future girlfriends, I have documentary evidence to back up my given answer to the question "So how did your last relationship end?")

But there are a few problems with that idea. First, though the iPhone has been out

for some months at this writing, Apple has yet to update iTunes so that it can synchronize desktop notes (like the ones you create in your Windows and Mac mail apps) to the iPhone. Dear God, you'd have to think that Apple will correct this sad state of affairs but for now, you're stuck having to tap, tap, tap all your trivia in manually.

That's too much work, particularly since most of the doo-dads you want to put on a digital device were digital to begin with: info that someone sent you via e-mail, stuff you found on the Web, etc. You'd rather just cut and paste this stuff.

Second, if you have an iPod Touch — the somewhat disadvantaged cousin to the iPhone — you can tap all you want but the Notepad app will not appear. It ain't there.

And thirdly, there's the usual hassle of iPhones and iPods: Your sole conduit for putting info on the device is a copy of iTunes on one specific computer. If someone tells you, "Oh, but if you're going to the Metropolitan Museum, don't go into the Egyptian wing on the first Tuesday of the month; that's when the moon god raises all the mummies from the dead and sends them on a rampage in a sickening harvest for human flesh" and you think, "Golly, I should probably have that info handy," you're out of luck if you aren't at the keyboard of your desktop computer at that moment.

Fortunately, both the iPhone and the iPod Touch have precisely the right tools for the job: a Web browser and Internet access. Or, to be more precise: the tools that we can use to *access* the right tool for the job.

I'LL TUMBLR FOR YA

Tumblr (www.tumblr.com) is a special kind of Weblog that's apparently been

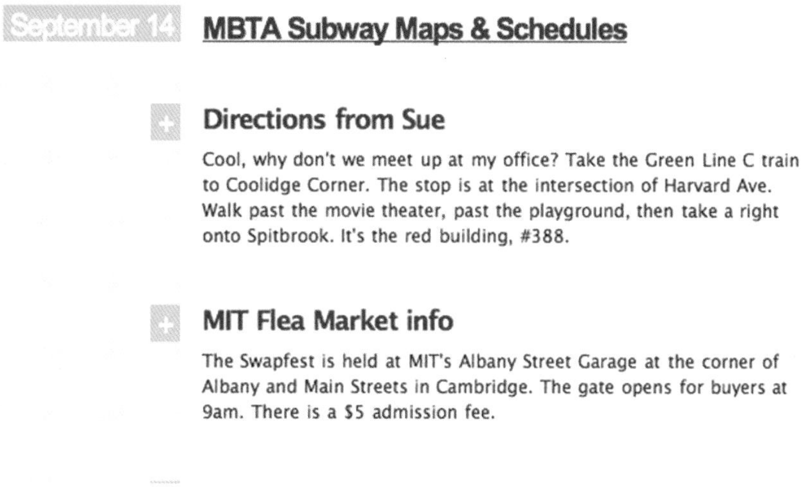

September 14 **MBTA Subway Maps & Schedules**

Directions from Sue

Cool, why don't we meet up at my office? Take the Green Line C train to Coolidge Corner. The stop is at the intersection of Harvard Ave. Walk past the movie theater, past the playground, then take a right onto Spitbrook. It's the red building, #388.

MIT Flea Market info

The Swapfest is held at MIT's Albany Street Garage at the corner of Albany and Main Streets in Cambridge. The gate opens for buyers at 9am. There is a $5 admission fee.

Figure 18-1
A Tumblr blog: lint trap for life's ephemera

dubbed a "microblog" by trouble-causing industry analysts who figure that there aren't *enough* confusing and annoying little buzz-words.

Whereas a "real" blog is for composing and publishing articles of any length with sophisticated formatting, a Tumblr blog allows you to share — yes, you guessed it — little doo-dads and clippings. Which is right up our street.

Figure 18-1 shows you a typical Tumblr blog as its founders intended it to be seen: in a Web browser, naturally.

If you squint, you'll note a few typical examples of the mental junk I'm talking about. You're going to be in Boston for the weekend. As luck would have it, the monthly MIT Flea Market is held that Sunday, so you go to the event Web page and clip the info about the place and time. Your pal Sue wants to get together for lunch; she's e-mailed you directions to her office via the subway.

TIP

Tumblr uses that e-mail address to associate you with your tumblelog. There's no real downside to using your "real" address for this, but there's no real upside, either. So you're probably better off visiting GMail or Yahoo (www.gmail.com, www.yahoo.com) and creating a brand-new (and free) e-mail account solely for your Tumblelog. The other upside of creating a new e-mail account is that more than one e-mail address means you can create more than one tumblelog. So you can have one as a "permanent" scrapbook, one just to collect the clippings you need for an upcoming event, one to share with friends, ... that sort of thing.

TIDBIT

This has next to nothing to do with iPhones or iPod Touches, specifically, but I should point out that there is indeed a flea market on the MIT campus on the third Sunday of every month, from April through October … and it's exactly as nerdy and wonderful as you're picturing it. You take one lap around the parking lot and garage full of technology — from consumer to military and laboratory, from antique to modern — and you think, "If I had an Apollo command module in my backyard and were trying to restore it, I'd come here looking for parts." Then you turn a corner and see a sign taped to the car of one of the vendors: "Looking for original parts to restore my Apollo Block I BP command module." No joke. I have photos.

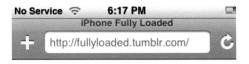

No Service   6:17 PM

iPhone Fully Loaded

http://fullyloaded.tumblr.com/

iPhone Fully Loaded

MBTA Subway Maps & Schedules

Directions from Sue

Cool, why don't we meet up at my office? Take the Green Line C train to Coolidge Corner. The stop is at the intersection of Harvard Ave. Walk past the movie theater, past the playground, then take a right onto Spitbrook. It's the red building, #388.

Figure 18-2
Tumbling into a handheld screen. Purty, innit?

And given that there's an entire classic folk song about a man who's been stranded for years on a constantly circulating MBTA train, it's probably a good idea to have a link to the system's online maps.

Tumblr doesn't offer an iPhone– or iPod Touch-specific page layout. But for Farfle's sake, it really doesn't need one. The standard layouts are bare-bones in design and they look just swell on an iPhone or iPod Touch screen (see Figure 18-2).

Tumblr has pre-set templates for four types of elements: text, pictures, links to Web pages, … and three others that probably aren't of any use to us here. Oh, all right: quotations, chat transcripts, and embedded videos from YouTube and other video-sharing sites.

SETTING UP A TUMBLELOG

Tumblr blogs (a.k.a. "tumblelogs") are free, free, free. To set yours up, all you need to do is visit www.tumblr.com and click the Sign Up link. Give Tumblr a valid e-mail address, make up a login password, and come up with a name to uniquely identify your tumblelog.

Once you've done that, Tumblr will take you to your tumblelog's "dashboard" (see Figure 18-3). You can change the appearance of your tumblelog and, more to the point, post new info to it.

From this point onward, any browser in the world can see what's on your tumblelog. If you named it "applepiehubbub" in the Register page, the URL would be http://

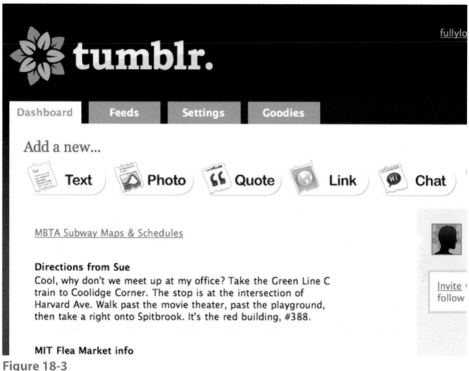

Figure 18-3
The Tumblr dashboard: where the info meets the road

applepiehubbub.tumblr.com. Bookmark this in your desktop browser and on your iPhone or iPod Touch; you'll be using it. A lot.

ADDING INFO TO YOUR TUMBLELOG

Unlike any other kind of blog, Tumblr was designed to be dead-simple to use and, gosh almighty, it accomplishes its mission. To post an item to your tumblelog:

1. Visit www.tumblr.com, click Log In, and type in the e-mail address and password you've associated with your tumblelog. Your tumblelog's dashboard will appear (again, see Figure 18-3).
2. Click the dashboard button for the type of item you'd like to add. Figure

18-4 shows you the online form for creating a new text post.

3. Give the new item a title and then type or paste in the text.
4. Click the Create Post button.

That's it. The new post is now on your tumblelog for all the world (but chiefly just you) to see.

You can post to your tumblelog from any computer anywhere. I mentioned the dead certainty that Apple will one day release a version of iTunes that can synchronize text between the iPhone's Note Pad app and your desktop information manager, but honestly, Tumblr is better in at least one way: I don't need to be in front of that one specific computer to "save" a clipping to my iPhone. If

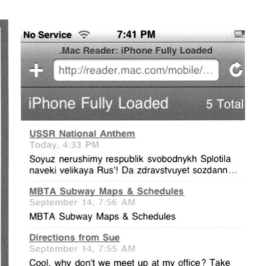

Figure 18-4
A more compact view of your clippings, via RSS

I'm at work, on a friend's computer, at a someone's office, it's all the same: access to a working Web browser = ability to post to my tumblelog.

If you click on the Goodies tab in the Dashboard, you'll turn up some alternative methods of posting to your tumblelog:

◗ Drag the Tumblr "bookmarklet" into your desktop Web browser's Bookmarks bar. From then on, any time you find yourself looking at a Web page that you'd like to keep handy in your tumblelog, just click the Share On Tumblr link in your browser window (see Figure 18-5). Some mojo hard-wired into the bookmark will grab that page's URL and turn it into a brand-new link post.

◗ You can also post items to your tumblelog directly from any e-mail client,

including the iPhone's Mail app. When you created your tumblelog, Tumblr generated a top-secret e-mail address for you that serves as a direct conduit. It's shown on the Goodies page. Any e-mail sent to this address (whether it's a new message or an e-mail you've received that you forward to the Tumblr address) will show up on your tumblelog. This e-mail address is made up of seemingly random letters and numbers, followed by "@tumblr.com," so it's probably best if you add it to your address book. But use this feature with extreme caution. On the surface it seems like it's a

Figure 18-5
A new spot of text for your online scrapbook

---

perfect way to "save" an e-mail you've received on one of your desktop e-mail accounts, do remember that (again) you're publishing it to the whole world, in effect. Even if the content isn't terribly personal, keep in mind that you might wind up exposing a friend or co-worker's private e-mail address to the world.

EDITING A POST

Now that you're home from Boston, maybe you feel like you'll never need any of the Boston-specific clippings you posted on your tumblelog ever again.

(As a lifelong Bostonian, well, that bothers me. Is there any particular reason why

you never want to return? Was it September when all the college kids come back to town? This is a time when many of these young men and women are exploring their first days free from the watchful eyes of their parents. I mean, normally, our streets aren't filled with quite so much pee, vomit, and loose teeth. Swear to God.)

Anything you post to your tumblelog can be edited or removed, right from the Dashboard. Just scroll down until you see the item you want to change and move your mouse into the item's airspace. A small palette of editing tools will magically appear in the item's upper-right corner (see Figure 18-7):

▸ Link isn't an editing thingy at all; it just contains a direct URL link to that

about images on Wikipedia •

Figure 18-6
The Tumblr bookmarklet lets you save a Web page's URL to your tumblelog with one click.

Figure 18-7
Who said there are no second chances? You can edit items you've posted to your tumblelog.

specific item. Copy this link if (say) you want a pal to know the phonetic lyrics to the Soviet national anthem. One e-mail and he can zap straight to it.

- The little pencil button in the middle opens the editing page, where you can modify the item's title and content.
- Click on the red X to remove the item permanently.

I sense that you're all very nice and understanding people. You're certainly not the sort who was thinking, "Oh, boy! Clippings!" when you started the chapter and immediately went sour on me when you found out that I was actually talking about posting items to a blog and reading it on the iPhone's or iPod Touch's Safari browser.

What can we say to such people, honestly? We can probably say, "You're precisely the type of person who, if you were drowning

and I threw you a life ring tied to a safety line, would immediately complain that I was hogging half of the rope for myself."

But we're solid, kindhearted folk, you and I. So instead we'd probably swallow our sarcasm and say, "This is actually a way better solution than using the Notepad. And remember, if you have an iPod Touch, you don't even *have* the Notepad app."

It takes all kind. But you know what? We have something those other people don't: a sense of smug arrogant superiority that comes from knowing that *we are so much better than them!*

19

Any Damned Information You Want

The Skim

I pledge allegiance to the iPhone and iPod Touch, and to the touch-screen for which they stand, ... etc., etc. By now you should appreci-ate that I like these devices. If they were bands, I would be hanging around outside the venue, angrily insisting the everyone there were just posers and *I* was a big fan back when they sold cassettes out of a guitar case on open-mic night at the 'Glade.

But I have one big problem with 'em: You have absolutely *zero* con-trol over what goes on the device. Any device like this that costs many hundreds of dollars should be an empty vessel into which I can decant any information I want to keep handy ... in addition to being a great phone, media player, and Internet appliance.

Regular iPods are bummers because (unlike most competing devices) you can't put any media on 'em unless you're physically sitting at the computer that hosts your iTunes library. But at least they have a "disk mode" and a special Notes folder. If you just want to carry a snippet of info with you (a complicated procedure for arming and disarming the alarm system at your new office, say) you can drag a text file into the folder and it's *there,* available for display at any time.

The iPhone and the iPod Touch are 100-percent closed, though. If

TIDBIT

The iPhone's Notes app is like a glass "Break in Case of Fire" cabinet with no fire extinguisher inside it. You look at it and you think, "Gosh, it sort of makes sense that Apple would (you know) allow you to synch actual *notes* into that app. Outlook has notes. The Mac OS Mail app has notes. What the … [choose a word]?" Again I bow down before you, oh mighty Reader of the Future. Here in my primitive times, we rise before the sun, we work in the fields for sixteen hours, we bring in the harvest, we sing and dance our rustic songs and dances, we make love, we give our thanks to an angry and indifferent god, we bury our dead, and then we begin the cycle anew. We are simple people and we as yet are not allowed to synch notes between our mail apps and iPhone Notes.

iTunes doesn't allow you to have something on your device, then it ain't gettin' in there.

What a sorry limitation. I want my iPhone to be many things, but first among them is for it to become the One Device. If you have the One Device, there's no need to carry a PDA or a separate music player or phone. You have a single reliable and powerful gizmo that can handle all your needs throughout the day.

Those needs are certain to include hundreds of things that Apple never considered.

The fact that you're not allowed to put your own information — regardless of form or format — on the iPhone or the iPod Touch is a serious limitation. But there are ways to work around it, ranging from the

simple to the clever to the downright ambitious. All these pursue the same two goals: (a) making *your own information* available via the iPhone and (b) being able to accomplish that without necessarily going through That Specific Computer Of Yours Running iTunes.

Deep breath now, because this might be a bit of a dark ride for the weak of heart. We'll start with the simple and sensible ideas and work our way deeper into the sludge pits as we go.

E-MAIL

Pros: Dead-simple; plain-text info is loaded directly on your iPhone; document files supported; can "add" information from any computer with an Internet connection.

Cons: Info is buried in your inbox; older e-mails are pushed out as new e-mails come in. Doesn't work with iPod Touch.

By far the easiest route into your iPhone's soul is the Mail app. By definition, it's an app that downloads any information and displays it, and it lets you squirm out from under the iron boot heel of international communism. I mean, of "iTunes." iTunes.

You can just e-mail information to your own usual e-mail account. But it's more convenient if your iPhone actually has its own separate e-mail account just for notes. That way, when you're walking around New York City and you want to refer to a list of used bookshops that you put together a few weeks ago for your upcoming trip, you'll be able to find it without having to slog through a hundred older messages.

It also makes it more likely that the info you sent yourself will still be there. Remember that the iPhone only keeps a limited number of messages in its internal storage. As new e-mails come in, old ones go away —

and they can be retrieved only if you have an active Internet connection.

Just head on over to www.yahoo.com or http://mail.google.com and get a free account for your iPhone. You can add this new account to your iPhone's usual round of mail downloads through the Settings button on your iPhone's application launcher.

And of course, this new conduit into your iPhone works from any computer anywhere. Just send an e-mail to theiphoneofkylemiller @yahoo.com (or whatever e-mail address you set up) and it'll land on the device.

And because the iPhone checks for mail and downloads messages automatically, the text of the message will be available to you whether you have an active connection to the Internet or not.

One tip, though: Go back into Mail's settings and under the Messages section, tell your iPhone to always show the maximum number of messages (which is 200, at this writing). If you have this set to the 25 (the minimum) as soon as your iPhone downloads its twenty-sixth message, the first message disappears. You'll be able to read it only if either the cell network or a Wi-Fi connection to the Internet is available.

And remember, the iPhone's built-in viewer for Word, Excel, HTML, and PDF files works in Mail. So if there's a spreadsheet full of information you want to have handy, e-mail it to yourself as an attachment.

You can even group together several related documents in a single e-mail, such as all of the info that's related to a specific business trip (see Figure 19-1).

ONLINE STORAGE

Pros: Supports every standard file format, including JPEGs, video, and music files; you

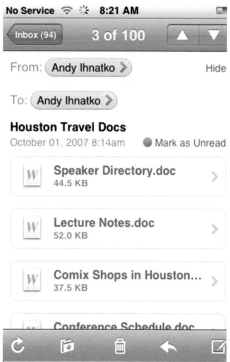

Figure 19-1

Putting travel docs together in a single e-mail, waiting in your inbox

can add files from any PC or Mac; files are well-organized and easy to access.

Cons: You can't get at your data unless you have an active Internet connection.

Apple gave us an unexpected boon when they incorporated the document reader in Safari. It's supposed to just help you read e-mail attachments, but because it's part of the browser, any Word, Excel, HTML or PDF file that's linked through the Safari window is also readable.

Which means that if you create an account on a service like Box (www.box.net), you can create a virtual thumb drive of documents that you can view any time you want — *if*

TIP

The best format for files that you intend to view on your iPhone or iPod Touch is HTML.

That's the standard format for Web pages, and it has a peculiar advantage because it's not designed for big sheets of paper.

Instead, it's designed for computer screens, and it's designed to let the viewer app (usually a browser) decide how best to display the text.

Figure 19-2 shows you what I mean.

On the left, you see the document presented as a Word file. The viewer is trying to approximate a sheet of paper, so the text is tiny and even if you zoom in, you'll have to keep scrolling side-to-side to read the text.

The HTML version on the right is much clearer because the viewer had the freedom to just do what it needs to do to make it read best.

Most modern word processors (including Word) have a built-in "save to HTML" feature.

It won't work with fancy formatting like multiple columns and running headers and footers, but it's perfectly fine for the sort of files you'll use for storing information.

Figure 19-2

Word docs (on the left) aren't nearly as convenient to read as HTML files (right).

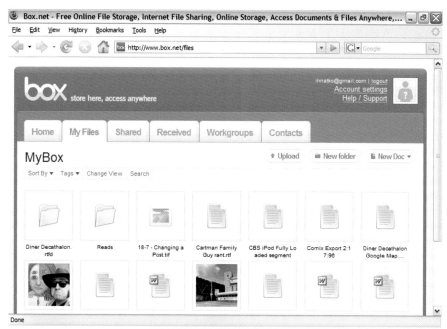

Figure 19-3
Box lets you "virtually" put any file you want onto your iPhone.

you have Internet access, of course.

You can sign up for a free account by visiting www.box.net in your desktop browser. You'll get a gigabyte of storage at no charge. If you pay for a subscription, you'll get more storage (as much as 10 gigabytes) and you'll be able to share files with friends and co-workers.

But one gig is plenty to keep our favorite files handy. Figure 19-3 shows Box in action. You can upload files into your online folder by logging in from any desktop browser and clicking the Upload button. You can even organize your files into subfolders, making it a snap to find the document you want on your iPhone. And by downloading a special helper app for your PC or Mac, you can even have your online storage appear on your desktop just like a "real" USB thumb drive.

There are lots of these online storage services but Box wins the prize for their terrific iPhone interface at http://i.box.net (see Figure 19-4). Just tap on a file or a folder to open it; if the file is in a format that the iPhone or iPod Touch supports, it'll open.

Among the many big wins of Box is that it works through the Safari browser. So you're not limited to just Word, HTML, Excel, and PDF files; you can also use it to store pictures, movies, and music files of any type supported by Safari's built-in media player.

"Amazing and astounding," you're saying, but I note a hint of sarcasm in your voice. Yes, I know: The iPhone and Touch already *have* meaty and wonderful apps for viewing and managing media files. Ah! But with Box you can make these files available to yourself *without having to go through iTunes!*

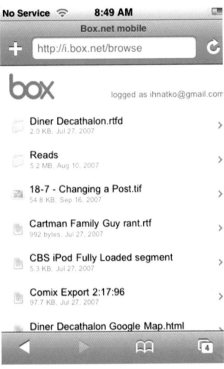

No Service 📶 8:49 AM

Box.net mobile

http://i.box.net/browse

logged as ihnatko@gmail.com

Diner Decathalon.rtfd
2.0 KB, Jul 27, 2007

Reads
5.2 MB, Aug 10, 2007

18-7 - Changing a Post.tif
54.8 KB, Sep 16, 2007

Cartman Family Guy rant.rtf
992 bytes, Jul 27, 2007

CBS iPod Fully Loaded segment
5.3 KB, Jul 27, 2007

Comix Export 2:17:96
97.7 KB, Jul 27, 2007

Diner Decathalon Google Map.html

Figure 19-4
Accessing your online files is a snap via Box's iPhone interface.

It's my main beef with the iPhone and iPods in general. How many times have I been visiting a pal and I've come across an *awesome* podcast or an interview or something online, something that's *perfect* for my two-hour drive home ... but I can't do anything with it because I don't have my Mac with me? *Lots* of times, that's how many.

But by just commandeering my pal's PC for five minutes, I can upload that 7 megabyte MP3 file into my Box folder. If I have my iPhone, I can just access Box and play the file right there in the car. So long as I have access to the cellular network, it'll play just fine; the built-in EDGE connection is

fast enough to stream an MP3. Not an MP4 video, sure, but I'm really not supposed to be watching video while I'm driving.

On an iPod Touch, I can still listen to the audio in my car. Before I leave that cozy bubble of Wi-Fi in my pal's office, I just access Box from my iPod Touch and tap on the MP3 file to start it playing. Then just pause it. The iPod Touch will buffer the whole file to local storage and so long as that Web page is up and active, it'll be playable.

Naturally, this is a great way not just for arbitrarily putting files on your iPhone or iPod Touch but also for saving storage space on your device. Some of you might even have those rare, original 4-gig iPhones — this will let you keep a gig of extra podcasts on the thing without taking up precious memory.

The other advantage of using Box.net to display your media instead of the iPhone's or iPod Touch's built-in apps? Photos. When you upload a 10-megapixel photo to Box, Safari lets you zoom in and view it at full resolution. Synch that photo into your iPhone's or iPod Touch's formal photo library and iTunes will automatically downgrade the photo to the resolution of your desktop screen.

Hmm. That gives me an idea ...

USING PHOTOS AS INFORMATION

Pros: Your data is written directly to your device, so it doesn't require an Internet connection; works with any type of data whatsoever; fancy formatting — including a combination of text and graphics — is supported.

Cons: You have to convert your documents to pictures; documents might not be terribly readable.

Let's think about this a moment. iTunes doesn't allow us to simply copy a document onto the device. So what sorts of stuff *can* it synch? Welp, it'll synch photos, and they say that a picture is worth a thousand words, right?

So all we need to do is convert a document into images. Then we synch those images to the iPhone or iPod Touch, and we can "read" them in the built-in photo viewer.

Before we talk techniques, you ought to know what sort of results we're going to get. Figure 19-5 shows you a Web page that I converted to a photo and then synched to the iPhone.

Yeah. Not exactly picture-perfect. But it's readable, at least. Unfortunately, iTunes does you a "favor" when it synchs images to the device: It downsamples the photo, reducing its resolution to make the file take up less space on the device.

It's very possible that you'll find that your docs are plenty readable when you synch them this way. But if you want perfection, if you want to be able to view the image at its full, original resolution … gosh, we'd need some way of accessing an arbitrary chosen file on our device, right?

Wait, didn't we just *talk* about something like that?

Yes, indeed. Figure 19-6 shows you that same document, except instead of synching it I uploaded it to my Box folder. *That's* more like it — and I didn't even save it as a print-resolution document. Of course, the advantage of iTunes doing the synch is that the document will be stored right on your device, but so long as you can count on an Internet connection, using Box is probably the better way to go.

Either way, your first step is to convert that document. It's actually pretty easy, thanks to a utility that allows you to "print" documents into JPEG files. It's a sweet technique because it'll work with any application that can print, which means — cool! — it works with any application.

Converting Documents to Images in Windows

My favorite tool for capturing all sorts of Windows data is TechSmith's SnagIt. Down-

The space shuttle Discovery land
mission: enter orbit, check to see
new hardware and techniques for
International Space Station to ke

It's hard not to imagine that we'v
process of rebuilding confidence
key problem with manned space
space is to certify that humans ca

It seems like we could skip a step
putting people up there to begin
we're getting better and better at
stuff on our behalf?

Yes, unmanned probes have had
nearsighted. The Mars Climate C
but wound up taking a dramatica

Figure 19-5
Docs as pictures: They lose a little something in the translation.

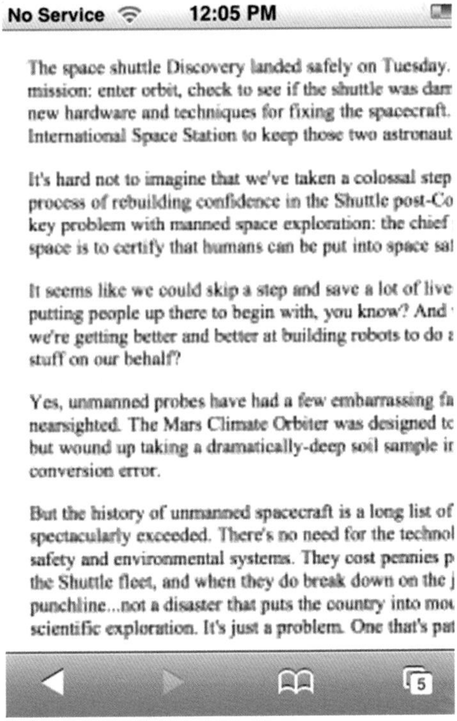

No Service 📶 12:05 PM

The space shuttle Discovery landed safely on Tuesday.
mission: enter orbit, check to see if the shuttle was dam
new hardware and techniques for fixing the spacecraft.
International Space Station to keep those two astronaut

It's hard not to imagine that we've taken a colossal step
process of rebuilding confidence in the Shuttle post-Co
key problem with manned space exploration: the chief
space is to certify that humans can be put into space saf

It seems like we could skip a step and save a lot of live
putting people up there to begin with, you know? And '
we're getting better and better at building robots to do a
stuff on our behalf?

Yes, unmanned probes have had a few embarrassing fa
nearsighted. The Mars Climate Orbiter was designed to
but wound up taking a dramatically-deep soil sample in
conversion error.

But the history of unmanned spacecraft is a long list of
spectacularly exceeded. There's no need for the technol
safety and environmental systems. They cost pennies p
the Shuttle fleet, and when they do break down on the j
punchline…not a disaster that puts the country into mou
scientific exploration. It's just a problem. One that's pat

Figure 19-6
Clarity of writing: viewing an imaged document via Box

load a free trial of the utility from www.
techsmith.com; if you want to keep it, it'll
cost you $39.

I love this app. It's slick, it's reliable, and
no matter what your capture-related problem, SnagIt contains the solution. In fact, I
was sort of banging my head a bit trying to
find a "print to JPEG" utility that I actually
liked. There are a bunch of 'em for Windows
but they're either grotesquely overpriced or
they don't work very well.

But I've been using SnagIt for years whenever I need to create a screen grab to accompany a book or article. I poked through its
menus for a bit and well, whaddyaknow?

Printer Capture is a built-in feature.
Here's how to get that feature going:

1. Launch the SnagIt application and
   click Setup SnagIt Printer in the main
   screen. This opens the SnagIt Printer
   Capture Settings dialog box.

2. Choose File from the Output pop-up
   menu. The SnagIt virtual printer will
   appear in every app's list of available
   printers. So let's create a brand-new
   one, specifically for the purpose of
   sending document into iTunes.

3. Click the Properties button next to
   Input. The Input Properties window
   now appears.

☑ Click the Add a SnagIt Printer button and give your new printer a name. Make it something snappy, like "Print to iPhone/iPod." SnagIt will grind for a moment and then tell you that it's been successfully added.

☑ Click OK to return to the Capture Settings dialog. Now we need to set it up so that it'll produce highly iPhone/Touch-friendly images.

4. Click the Properties button next to the Output pop-up menu to open the Output Properties window. It should open directly in the Image File tab.

☑ Under File Format, click Always Use This File Format and then JPG – JPEG Image.

☑ Under File Name, click Ask For File Name.

☑ Under Folder, check Always Use This Folder and then specify a folder for the captured documents. Create a special folder just for captures.

☑ Click OK to return to the Capture Settings dialog box.

5. Choose Image Resolution from the Filters pop-up menu. Uncheck the Auto Configure option and enter "96" in the Resolution (dots per inch) box. This will create images that are identical to the resolution of your screen. If you're working with detailed docs (with lots of text), you might want to increase the setting to fax resolution (200 dpi) or even printer-resolution (300 dpi). But this will result in very beefy image files and you'll only be able to see the higher resolution if you're using Box to store the images instead of using iTunes to store them directly on your device.

Figure 19-7

Printing to your virtual printer

6. Click OK to close the Image Resolution settings box and then again to close the Capture Settings dialog box. Your fake printer is now ready to roll. To print using your new fake printer:

1. Select the Print command from any application, such as by choosing File ▶ Print or pressing ⌘+P.

2. Choose the SnagIt printer that you created earlier (see Figure 19-7). SnagIt will show you a brief progress bar as it captures the printer output. When it's done, it'll alert you via the taskbar.

3. Click the flashing SnagIt Capture Preview window in the taskbar to open it. SnagIt shows you a preview of what it's captured.

4. Click SnagIt's Finish (File) button at the top of the Preview window to save this converted document to your designated folder. SnagIt will take you to its Save Multiple Images dialog box. If you have a three-page document, naturally SnagIt will save three separate JPEG files. You've already configured this printer with the settings you want, so now all you need to do is give this sequence a name to remember it by.

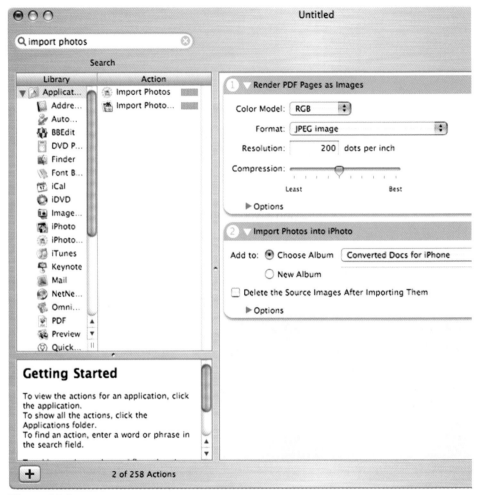

Figure 19-8
Automator lets you add your own "Print to iPhone" feature to your Mac.

5. Name the file something pithy in the File Name Prefix box and click OK.

That's it. The JPEG files will appear in the designated folder.

To load them on your device, see Chapter 20 for instructions on synching images. If you're using Box to view this stuff, just upload the JPEG files directly into a folder on your online storage.

Converting Documents to Images on a Mac

The good news is that you don't need to buy anything to print documents to a series of JPEGs. The *bad* news is that a tiny amount of manual labor is involved.

The Mac OS includes a wonderful utility called Automator that allows you to automate simple tasks. You'll find this miraculous wonder mop in the Applications folder. Or just look for the Dock icon that depicts a robot holding a potato bazooka. Apple says he's just holding a pipe, thus reminding you that the motif of this app is that you're connecting pre-baked functions together, but don't be fooled. It's a potato cannon. That boy's getting himself into mischief, just mark my words.

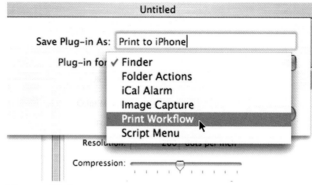

Figure 19-9

Saving a workflow so that it's available in every Print dialog box

You need to tell Automator that you want it to perform a two-step process:

- First, it should transmogrify PDF-formatted data (like the kind that Mac's standard Print feature generates) into image files.
- Second, it should import those files into iPhoto.

Automator contains a huge library of pre-built functions. Your only task is to snap these together in the order you want, like a stack of Legos. When you're done, you'll have a beast known as a "workflow." Figure 19-8 shows you a "Print to iPhone" workflow.

Here's how to build it:

1. Create a new workflow by pressing ⌘+N or choosing File ▶ New. The first action you need is the Render PDF Pages As Images action. The easiest way to find it is via Automator's Search box, located in the upper-left corner of the window.

2. Click the search field and type "Render PDF Pages." That's more than enough to locate the action. Automator will list the action in the Action column of the window.

3. Drag the Render PDF Images action into the workflow area on the right side of the window. This action has a bunch of options available; you can choose what format you want (choose JPEG) and how much detail you want the image to have (choose 72 if you're content with screen resolution, 200 if you want something closer to print-quality detail). This action spits out JPEG files. We want those JPEGs to wind up in the hands of Automator's Import Photos into iPhoto action.

4. Search for "Import Photos into iPhoto" and drag the action into the workflow space, under the Render PDF Pages action. See what happened? The two actions automatically made a connection. The PDF action creates JPEGs, the Import action accepts JPEGs. Done and dusted!

5. Select a photo album to receive any pages created by this workflow. You'll probably want to create a brand-new album, just so that it's easy to keep these pages organized. Believe it or

not, you now have a working "Print to iPhone" feature. Now, you just need to wire it into your Mac's standard Print dialog box.

6. Another piece of cake: You can save Automator workflows as plug-ins, integrating them into other parts of your Mac. To do so, choose File ▶ Save as Plug-In.

7. From the Save dialog box that appears, choose Print Workflow (see Figure 19-9). Give the plug-in a snappy name and click OK.

Congrats: All your Mac apps can now print to your iPhone. To use this intensely neat new feature:

1. Select Print from any app. The standard Print dialog box appears.

2. Select Print to iPhone (or whatever you named it) from the PDF pop-up menu.

Bingo. The Automator workflow takes it from there and the printed pages will land directly in your iPhoto library. So long as this iPhone photo album is synched to your device via iTunes, your documents will be installed on your iPhone.

If you've chosen to use Box to manage and view these docs (so that you can see them at full resolution), you'll need to export them from iPhoto first. Just select the album and choose File ▶ Export.

CONVERTING DOCUMENTS TO AUDIO

Pros: Can run through your data and documents in the car without causing an airbag deployment.

Cons: A fiddly process, and there's no skimming allowed: A 500-word document takes five minutes to listen to all the way through.

I've shown you the trick of converting documents to pictures that iTunes can then synch to the iPhone's or iPod Touch's photo library. How about converting them to audio, so iTunes can synch 'em like any other MP3 file?

You can't be serious.

Actually, sure, you can. That's no way to run through quick memos, but if you've been handed a long contract or boring report that you *must* check through, listening to it as audio could be a better way of spending your two-hour commute than listening to a two-CD Abba greatest-hits collection.

Definitely. A report on the bid process for the new desalinization contract is *definitely* better than Abba.

The easiest way to convert documents to speech is with the $30 iAudioize from Magnetic Time (www.magnetictime.com). It converts e-mails and documents into MP3

TIP

In Chapter 11, I had a rant about the ongoing passion play of third-party iPhone and iPod Touch apps. Apple doesn't want 'em but developers want to write 'em. The state of these apps is in flux (Apple has updated the iPhone firmware so that these apps can't be installed, but clever people have ways to make them run anyway).

Nonetheless, I'm eager to tell you that there's a wonderful little app called Book that reads Text and HTML documents of any length. Figure 19-10 shows it in action, with all the little buttons that let you tailor the display to your own strengths and weaknesses as a person of sight; you can make those buttons go away, leaving just a full screen of text.

Here I'm reading Mark Twain's *Innocents Abroad*, which ain't no teensy little file that explains the dress code at your new office. It's a whole freakin' book.

But Book works great with any kind of data, long– or short-form. And because it reads files that are stored right on your iPhone, you can access this text whether there's an Internet connection or not. You can read it on a train, you can read it on a plane. You can read it here or there …

Anyway. Visit http:// code.google.com/p/ iphoneebooks for more info on installing and using Book. And, read Chapter 11 for more info on getting your iPhone or iPod Touch to run third-party apps to begin with.

audio using clear, natural speech. I talk about this app in greater detail in Chapter 21, but converting documents is really just a three-step process:

1. Click the Documents button at the lower-left corner of the iAudioize window.

2. Open the document you want to read. iAudioize supports both Word and plain-text documents. iAudioize will add the document to its queue.

3. Click the iPod button (in Windows) or the Export button (on the Mac) at the top-right of the screen. iAudioize will convert the documents (along with whatever e-mails you've selected) into MP3 files and add them to a special playlist in your iTunes library.

Cool; just tell iTunes to keep this playlist synched to your iPhone or iPod Touch and every morning will be filled with bumper-to-bumper I-95 traffic and the thrilling verbiage of a man with a degree in law and a minor in engineering explaining why metal-lurgical tests on the DiscoHeart 2000 surgical valve replacement have demonstrated that cost-efficiency versus reliability of this component has sunk to an unacceptable level based on RSG.

I keep thinking back to George Carlin's "A Place for My Stuff" routine. He talks about how a house is, in truth, just a big pile of stuff with a cover on it. And every time you leave it (from the house to a hotel in Hawaii, from the hotel to a local friend's house for the weekend, from the friend's house to a full 24 hours on the beach, sleeping in the car), you keep having to create an *even smaller* version of "your stuff."

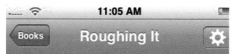

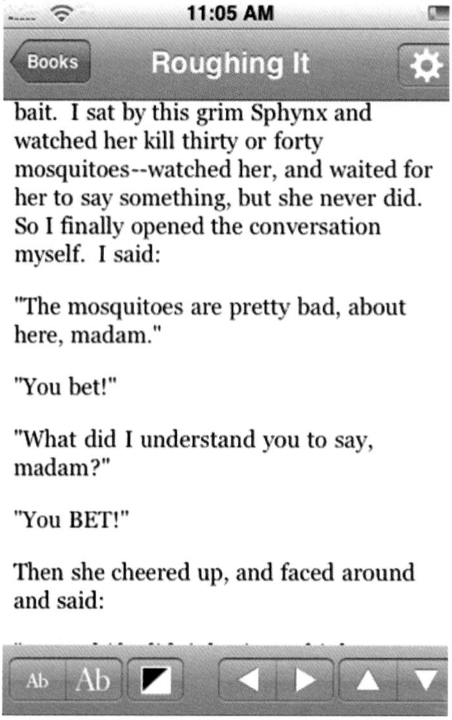

11:05 AM

Books   **Roughing It**   ⚙

bait. I sat by this grim Sphynx and watched her kill thirty or forty mosquitoes--watched her, and waited for her to say something, but she never did. So I finally opened the conversation myself. I said:

"The mosquitoes are pretty bad, about here, madam."

"You bet!"

"What did I understand you to say, madam?"

"You BET!"

Then she cheered up, and faced around and said:

Figure 19-10
Book, a third-party book reader for the iPhone

I have about three terabytes of storage on my home network. When I travel, I take a notebook with a 120-gig hard drive and a portable 250-gig drive. When it's too hot to work inside my air conditioning-free office (no, I'm not doing it to be "green"; I'm just cheap), I take the notebook to the library.

But I *always* have my iPhone with me. And that makes the iPhone into the *ultimate* place for my stuff. It's the smallest thing I carry, but that means the things I keep on it are the most important things imaginable.

20

Picture That

The Skim

Moving Pictures ◼ Narrowing the Synch

Oh, what a paradise the world must have been back in 1861. Yes, the country was beset with strife and would soon be rent in two by the bloodiest war in American history. Oh, and routine pandemics of cholera, a child mortality rate that's mind-boggling by any standard, total lack of any sort of middle class plus a lower class that had the rights, opportunities, and overall quality of life as medieval serfs.

Right, good points.

What makes me slightly fond for those days was the fact that getting a family picture taken required people to travel quite a long distance, spend about three months' worth of wages, and convince their children to sit for eight minutes with their bodies kept rock-still by iron frames that screwed onto bones.

As a result, you didn't tend to be accosted with these things back in those days. Maybe twice a year. I may be a twisted little misanthrope, but I can still fake a smile and say, "Ohhh, isn't she *adorable!*" in reaction to just one or two photos, particularly when they're spaced several months apart.

Even in the 20th century, things weren't *too* bad. Sure, you could get tricked into sitting through a vacation slideshow. *Once.* But once bitten, twice shy: As soon as you followed your host into the rec room and saw that there was a cover on the pool table and a screen erected on the wall across from the sofa, you were wise enough to deliver a sharp elbow to his solar plexus and flee through the kitchen while he's scrabbling on the floor and dealing with double vision.

We have all been completely screwed by digital photography. New parents can shoot hundreds of pictures a *day*. And devices like the iPhone and the iPod Touch mean that they're all loaded into their pockets *automatically*, ready to be inflicted upon an innocent bystander like yourself at a moment's notice without even the pretense of remorse.

I urge you folks to use this feature cautiously. And if (like me) you don't have kids of your own, I suggest that you use this feature in a defensive capacity. "I'd *love* to see that 238-photo slideshow of little Morton's fourth-grade graduation," you can say, unholstering your own iPhone. "But first, wouldn't you like to see some photos of my father's recent bile duct operation?"

MOVING PICTURES

iTunes is normally the warehouse that holds all your iPhone and iPod Touch's potential inventory. But there's a snag, here: iTunes happily will manage your music and your videos, but although it's charitably willing to acknowledge the existence of these things known as "pictures," it's not willing to store or organize them for you.

So iTunes offers you a Willy Wonka-land like assortment of colorful options and features for loading music and videos on your device, but when it comes to pictures all you can do is tell iTunes where, specifically, to get those photos from and how you'd like them stored on your device.

I shall continue the Wonka metaphor and describe the iPhone Options window as the big colorful candyland area with the chocolate river that Augustus Gloop tumbles into (see Figure 20-1). Like the movie set, this window is central to the entire operation.

You can open your iPhone's or iPod Touch's options by just clicking its name in iTunes's Devices list.

Click the Photos tab to change the photo settings. By default, the Synchronize Photos From feature is unchecked, meaning that iTunes won't bother slapping pictures onto your device.

To turn on photo synchronization, click the checkbox. Next tell iTunes where to synchronize photos *from*. This boils down to two choices:

- ◖**A handy-dandy, nicely organized formal photo library.** Managed by a slick application that slurps pictures straight from your camera and slaps baby pictures into printed calendars faster than your friends can throw them away.
- ◖**Any old folder.** Which is just what you think it means. You point iTunes at a folder and zap: Pictures in the folder become pictures on your device, automagically. If there are subfolders in there, the subfolders will appear as albums in the iPhone's or iPod Touch's photo viewer.

From Photo Libraries

This is clearly the smoothest way to go, because that's how you naturally tend to organize your pictures on your computer. The simplest way of managing photos on an iPhone or iPod Touch is to just let your photo library do most of the heavy lifting for you.

But, there's bad news. The relationship between iTunes and a photo library manager is a fairly intimate one and, as such, iTunes won't work with just *any* application. For a Mac user, well, you definitely want to use iPhoto. It came with your computer, it works well, and when you plug anything that even *smells* like a digital camera into your

Figure 20-1
Setting your iPhone's photo preferences

Mac, the OS has already been configured to automatically hand the microphone off to iPhoto and cue up a Tony Bennett record, so to speak.

It's a bad news/exceptionally good news situation on the Windows side. PCs don't all ship with the same library app, and furthermore, there isn't *one* insanely popular app that everybody uses (like iPhoto on the Mac). But Adobe has a terrific photo library manager called Adobe Photoshop Elements. It's a "junior" edition of Photoshop with a

bodacious collection of editing and organizational tools, including a photo library manager.

It's a commercial product, but it's cheap ($100). And if "cheap" is too much money for you, Adobe also offers a free (free, free) app that's just a photo library manager and a basic editor: Adobe Photoshop Album Starter Edition. You can download it from www.adobe.com.

Whether you're using a PC or a Mac, an Adobe product, iPhoto, or some other

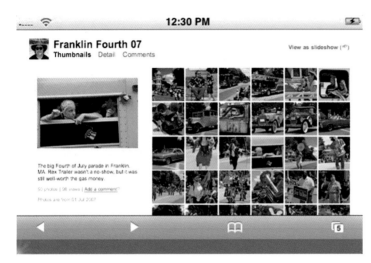

Figure 20-2
Break through storage problems and add lots of photo features beside, by using Flickr as your photo viewer.

library manager, all "eligible" photo apps will appear in the pop-up menu of iTunes's photo settings panel.

From any Old Folder

You can tell iTunes to synch pictures from any folder attached to your computer. The Choose Folder option is straightforward enough that I'm only going to haul out the numbered-list format because I set up my word processor with a special button that generates them automatically:

1. Choose the Choose Folder option from the pop-up list.
2. Navigate to the folder you'd like iTunes to synchronize from, and click OK.

iTunes populates this pop-up list with your OS's most likely spot for storing pictures: My Pictures for the Windows kids and Pictures for the Mac gang. But it can be any directory your machine can see, even a remote folder on a network that everyone in the office uses as a collective photo dump.

NARROWING THE SYNCH

By default, iTunes selects the Copy All Photos and Albums option, which means it'll attempt to copy the whole kit and caboodle when it synchs. This is a Good Thing if you have no heart whatsoever and you really believe that you're going to find a willing audience for (good Lord) 8,963 of your personal photos.

I mean, honestly. You're already pushing it with thirty or forty. There's maybe one good reason for making somebody sit through a slide show of hundreds or thousands of pictures, and even if you *do* find yourself in that sort of a position, you can usually get a confession out of the prisoner a lot faster by simply dropping your iPhone into a sock and beating him with it. You really want to pare down the number of photos on your device before it lands you in trouble with the World Court as well as with karma.

There are more obvious reasons, of course. Photos take up space on your iPhone that could be filled with more Dan Fogelberg music (though again, the iPhone-in-a-sock technique a more effective means of torture and is considered to be more humane as well).

Plus, lots of photos cost you lots of time. iTunes has to prep and copy each picture. Go ahead and show up late for work. Explain to

TIDBIT

The *best* solution might be to leave photos off your iPhone entirely. And not just from the perspective of your friends or relatives, either.

I'm an *enormous* fan of Flickr, an online photo album site. You upload your photos from your desktop straight into a private space on www.flickr.com, and view and share your photos on any computer with an Internet connection.

Even if you don't use any of the third-party Flickr tools available for the iPhone or iPod Touch, the basic Flickr screen looks fine on an iPhone or iPod Touch (take a gander at Figure 20-2).

I have nearly 3,000 photos on my Flickr feed (www.flickr.com/photos/andyi), which means that I have pocket access to nearly every neat event or observance of the past five years.

The other coolness of

Flickr is that you can post items to your Flickr album straight from your iPhone. Flickr gives you a free e-mail address that serves as the conduit.

If you run into Angela Lansbury at the tire store, all your friends and family can see the happy picture minutes later via the Camera app's Share via E-Mail feature.

your boss that you missed your train because it took iTunes ten minutes to update your iPhone this morning with the 320 photos you shot of your dog trying to do his little trick last night. See if *that* sort of attitude helps you get your name on the corporate letterhead.

Unless my advice means nothing to you, click the Copy Selected Albums/Folders Only option to tell iTunes to only copy a subset of your picture collection to the iPod during each synch.

Good: I'm glad my words are sinking in. Whether you're synching to a photo library or to a folder, iTunes offers you the same option for selecting elements of your picture collection. The list contains all of the photo albums in your photo library, or all of the subfolders inside the folder you picked (see Figure 20-1).

Select as few or as many as you like by clicking their checkboxes.

You can also drag these items around to change their order, whether you're synching every folder or album or just a few selected items. Selected albums or folders nearer to the top of the list will be synchronized before the ones at the bottom. This is a big deal if (if?! more like *when*) your iPhone or iPod Touch is running low on free space.

See, iTunes doesn't even *pretend* that it loves pictures the same way it loves music and videos. Dr. Phil would have a *fit* if he learned about this poisonous family dynamic. When iTunes synchs your device, it first copies all the tunes and vids and only then does it grudgingly fill any leftover space with pictures.

So if you care about which pix wind up on your device and which ones might get left behind, put the most important albums and photos at the top. My iPhone is usually set to synch the following albums, in this order:

1. An album of must-haves: the pictures that I always want to have on my

TIDBIT

I miss a certain feature of the regular iPods that's missing on the iPhone and the iPod Touch: You can't store photos at full resolution. iTunes will downsample each of your pictures before it's loaded onto your device, resulting in an image that contains a quarter as much detail as the original — if that.

What did *we* do to annoy Apple? These devices have big screens and can zoom, zoom, zoom in as far as we like. So why hamstring us with lower-resolution photos?

Granted, there's still enough detail for casual photo showin' and even comic readin'. Figure 20-3 shows you what iTunes does to your photos. As you can see, you're missing out on a *lot*.

Figure 20-3
Argh. iTunes throws out a lot of detail before throwing a photo on your iPhone. Compare the iPhone's version (top inset) versus the original image (bottom inset).

device, no matter what. (You think I'm going to leave the house without the photo of me and the "Time to make the donuts" guy from the Dunkin' Donuts commercial? As if.)

2. A "smart album" that always contains the 36 photos that have been added to the library most recently.

3. Whatever albums reflect recent family events and other cool news that are likely to come up in conversation.

4. Comic books. What, you didn't know that you could use your iPhone or iPod Touch as a comic book reader? Sounds to me like you skipped over Chapter 8.

5. Everything else. This is why I always check All Photos and Albums. What's the point of carrying around an iPhone or an iPod Touch that has *empty space* left on it? That's anathema to the glorious mission of this book. Because photos are always the last things to be synched, this means that they'll fill up the remaining megabytes with whichever ones fit.

So I get the best of both worlds. If last weekend's Newport Chowder Cook-Off happens to come up in conversation, I can whip out a photo of my friend John and his stack of 40 empty cups to convince any doubters. And a man who walks with a photo of himself sitting in the Batmobile, even one taken three years ago, walks with quiet power and serenity.

I have the new pix and the important pix, and I leave the rest at home. Not coincidentally, I still have friends who are willing to hang out with me and who don't mind terribly if I start scrolling through pictures with my handheld.

Okay, well, I guess I *should* acknowledge that for many members of our society —

folks who have kids, I suppose; more and more states are passing laws allowing that sort of thing — having lots of pictures in your pocket and being able to unholster them at a moment's notice is a *good* thing. And I should also point out that you can buy a special cable that lets you plug your iPod Touch straight into a TV, so that a whole living room full of folks can enjoy the show.

But again I say: Please use this power for *good,* not *evil.* I should also clarify that I'm not hostile toward your showing me pictures of your kids, friends, or the high-ticket consumer items that are currently acting as shabby substitutes for same.

I encourage you to bring 'em out *after* you've filled me with barbecue and *before* you've brought out the pies. I'm already in a genial and grateful mood and there's also the chance that if I refuse to show proper enthusiasm for your photo essay of the time little Bonfiglio and Iasolde made a bust of Herman Melville out of lawn clippings, I might not get any pie.

21

E-Mail

The Skim

Egalitarian E-Mail Tips ■
Turning E-Mails into Podcasts

As a little kid in school, I *prayed* that every social interaction could be like e-mail.

"Is this seat taken?" Ann Malloy asked me in the lunchroom on the first day of fourth grade. If she'd e-mailed me about it instead, I'd have read it on my sofa, or maybe while having a bowl of Frosted Flakes — you know, a place where I felt safe and secure. I could have read and re-read it over and over again to try to evaluate every possible meaning from those four words, and worked out every possible *response,* and then evaluated every possible response that *she* could make to my response. And a cozy three hours later, I'd finally click Send on the draft I'd been working on all morning.

As things were, I think I blurted out, "If you're worried about the pee smell, it wasn't me; I think it was that kid in the Patriots jersey who just left."

You see why I'm rather fond of this alternative method of communication.

An iPhone has a lovely e-mail client built in. The iPod Touch has no e-mail client, but it *does* have an Internet connection. And where there's Wi-Fi, there's hope.

Either way, there are interesting ways to articulate your e-mail. As usual, it just takes cash and effort.

EGALITARIAN E-MAIL TIPS

Let me dole out one simple tip for each of you. Just so you don't think I'm favoring one of you over the other, I recommend that both of you sign up for a free e-mail account on GMail or Yahoo.

iPhone Users: Get a "Desk Drawer" E-Mail Account

The iPhone's built-in mail client is indeed quite nice, but it's by no means a power tool. My inbox has such a great gravitational pull that most of my life tends to orbit around it. I'm flying to Houston shortly to give a talk; all the important details of the trip have arrived via e-mail.

On my desktop client, I have a special folder for that stuff. If I don't move it into the Keepers folder, information about who's picking me up at the airport will quickly get buried under the hundreds of e-mails I get a week. That's a particular concern on the

iPhone, which can only hold the most recent 200 messages in your inbox.

A day or two later, I'll need that piece of data but dang ... it's already been bumped out of my iPhone's inbox by mail from strangers who insist that my CI4L1S Prescr1pt1on is ready. If I don't have an Internet connection available, I'm hosed.

That's why I have a whole separate e-mail "keeper" account on my iPhone. It's a free account on http://mail.yahoo.com (Google's GMail would have worked just as well). Every time I get a message that's important enough to keep, I just tap the mail app's Reply button, tap Forward, and direct it to my "keeper" mail account.

In a few minutes, it arrives in the iPhone inbox for my "keeper" mail account. And because I only use that address for forwarding e-mails that I want to save, it never contains more than my most recent and most important messages. If one of these messages is old enough to be bumped from the bottom of the list, but it's too useful to lose, it's no trouble at all: I just forward it again, straight back to the "keeper" address. Voilà, it's back at the top of the list.

iPod Touch Users: Get a Web Mail Address!

I was actually a bit surprised when Apple announced the iPod Touch and described all its features ... but it turned out that the device wouldn't ship with the iPhone's e-mail client.

I mean, an iPod with Wi-Fi and Safari is great. But one with Wi-Fi, Safari, and Mail would have been *awesome.*

But it's kind of a waste to have such a slick, modern Wi-Fi device and not get mail on it. So go to http://mail.yahoo.com or www.

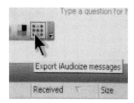

Figure 21-1
The magic button that sends your speakable e-mail from Outlook to iAudioize

Figure 21-3
E-mail waits in iAudioize's queue until you click the Export button.

TURNING E-MAILS INTO PODCASTS

There's another keen little tip that you can use whether you have an iPhone or an iPod Touch: You can convert your e-mail into a spoken-word podcast automatically.

(Humor me.)

(Look, you've already paid for the book. You might as well just keep on reading.)

I receive what I feel is a very manageable volume of e-mail. Not everyone does. It sometimes comes in by the double bucketful, as though you fell on the wrong end of that scene in *The Sorcerer's Apprentice*, where the magic broomsticks just keep bringing in buckets of water whether you want 'em to or not.

Problem 2 in your life is that you have a pretty long commute every morning. Problem 3 is that people tend to e-mail important stuff at all hours, and Problem 4 is that you really need to arrive

Figure 21-2
E-mail is lined up in iAudioize and is ready to be transmogrified.

gmail.com and sign up for a free e-mail account. Both services allow you to access your inbox via a special Web page, and they both work fine on the iPod Touch.

And you can set it up to function just like your "real" e-mail account, too. GMail, for instance, has a special mail app within the mail app. If you provide it with your main account's login details, Gmail will automatically log into the account at regular intervals and copy your new messages into your GMail account's inbox. (Yahoo Mail can do the same.)

at the office with a game plan for the day, knowing in advance what you need to dread.

You also don't rate a company car and driver. So reading e-mails while you drive is medically contraindicated.

(Criminy. It sucks to be you. Do you have a five-year plan? Because every time I hear people talk about jobs like this, they tell Oprah how they finally had enough, quit the 9-to-5, opened a cupcake shop in Peterboro, New Hampshire, and now find themselves atop an international baking empire. Something to think about. Wouldn't you like to be

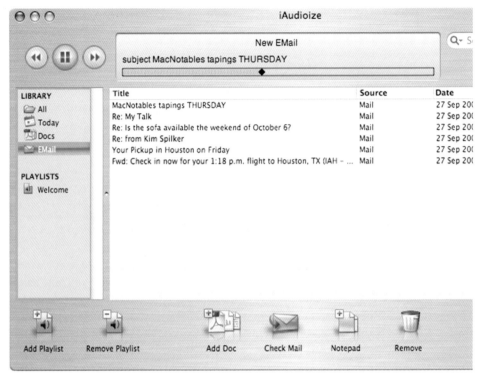

Figure 21-4
Mac messages awaiting conversion

on the Oprah show? I sure would.)

Well, there's a slick tool — available in both Mac and PC editions — that can take your incoming mail messages and automatically convert them to smooth, natural-sounding human speech. It's called iAudioize. It's forty bucks and is produced by a company called MagneticTime (www.magnetictime.com). Head on over and download a free, functioning demo.

Both editions of the app work in the same general fashion, with a few individual quirks. After you've installed iAudioize, you'll find a new mail folder (MagneticTime for Outlook, iAudioize for Mac Mail). iAudioize will grab messages from this mail folder; any-

thing that lands in this folder will ultimately be processed into spoken text.

For this reason, you need to use Outlook or Mail's rules feature to define the types of e-mails that should be redirected or copied into this folder. I'm angry enough as it is when I just have to read the subject lines of spam; if I'm forced to listen to the heart-breaking letter of a cancer-stricken Nigerian oil prince, well, no good can come of it.

So set up rules that fill this special folder with mail that you know are important and worthy of your attention during your commute or daily jog.

The process for converting e-mail differs between PC and Mac. On the PC:

1. Click the iAudioize button that the app attached to your Outlook toolbar when iAudioize was installed (see Figure 21-1). The messages will be moved into iAudioize's main window for processing (see Figure 21-2). They'll appear in a tidy list, complete with subject lines, so you can get a sense of what you're about to convert.

2. Uncheck any e-mail that you don't want converted.

3. Click the iPod button in the top-right corner of the window to convert all the e-mail into MP3s and send them into your iTunes library (see Figure 21-3).

Things are actually a bit simpler on the Mac. The Mac iAudioize app automatically checks Mail's iAudioize folder for new messages, and copies them into its main window without you clicking any buttons. Figure 21-4 shows you a batch of messages lined up in iAudioize, awaiting processing:

1. Open the iAudioize app. All the e-mail directed to your iAudioize folder appear in the list.

2. Remove any messages that you don't want converted by selecting them and clicking the Remove button at the bottom of the window.

3. Click the Export button to convert your e-mail to audio files and send them into your iTunes library.

No matter which version you used, the result is the same: a stack of individual MP3 files in your iTunes library. By default, they'll be organized into a new playlist called iAudioize-Emails. iAudioize tags its files by setting the Artist to iAudioize. So it's quite easy to build an iTunes smart playlist that chooses just the e-mail that has been received within the past day, for instance.

> **TIP**
>
> If certain e-mails are so important that you'd like to keep 'em on your iPhone or iPod Touch just as independent free-floating Molecules of Information, both Outlook and Mail (and any other mail client, really) can export your e-mail as text files … and then the techniques outlined in Chapter 19 allow you to install 'em on your device permanently.

E-mail is your shadow. The faster you run from it, the faster it follows you and the longer the day gets, the longer your inbox seems to be.

But after you accept it as a fact of life (like "nothing halfway good on TV on Wednesday night") and bring a little creativity to your approach, you'll find ways to bend e-mail to your will.

22

Spreadsheets and Databases

The Skim

Spread 'Em for Google ■ EditGrid to the Rescue ■
Onward to Databases

Databases are the brazil nuts of the iPhone Supported Data Types
Mixed Fancy Cocktail Nuts Assortment. Ignored, unloved, chucked
at your little brother when no other means of communicating the sen-
timent "I don't care whose turn it is; you can have the Wii when I'm
done with it, and not before" seems to be working.

At least in the eyes of the iPhone development team members. They
included great support for Microsoft Word and Excel documents: If
someone e-mails one of those things to you, or if you encounter a link
to one on a Web page, it'll open and display the doc, no sweat.

But you're on your own with database information. That's a shame,
given how much corporate and even personal data is managed by
database apps. You can see their logic, though. I have my own favorite
database app (FileMaker Pro for both PC and Mac), but in truth there
are four or five popular formats and there's no 900-pound-gorilla in the
category.

So if you want to carry your comic book collection with you — huh?
Your boss is watching and you put this book on your expense account?

Oh, sorry ... sorry.

If you're trying to maximize your lead-conversion percentage and hit

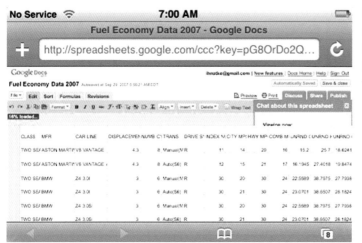

Figure 22-1
A big ol' spreadsheet, opened in Google Docs

all your targets by maintaining up-to-date metrics of client and lead data from your company's bid database, you'll have to massage the data yourself.

SPREAD 'EM FOR GOOGLE

But first, a bit of musing on the subject of spreadsheets. The iPhone has been out for a few months now and I am starting to think

TIDBIT

I have had my heart broken and rebroken over and over again in the few short months since the iPhone was released.

A long sequence of lotharios have toyed with my emotions time and time again and I never seem to learn to stop trusting people who claim that they've developed online apps that allow iPhone users to create and edit Microsoft Office documents.

"C'mon ... surely you've heard of gOffice.com?" you snort. "Or Zoho.com? Or ... "

Stop right there. Yes, I've tried them all, at least up to this writing, and *none of them work.*

Either they can just *read* Office docs but not edit them or, worse, they made a few bare, superficial changes to their generic service's user interface to make it *somewhat* useful for the iPhone.

Honestly, they don't give the appearance of an online app carefully designed to provide a terrific user experience for iPhone owners.

They look like some minor changes to an existing Office site's style sheets so that they could issue a press release and maybe piggyback on the publicity for the iPhone.

I hope things will have changed by the time you read this (anywhere from six weeks to two years from today) but for now ... I'm like Oliver Hardy, giving up the ways of love forever and joining the French Foreign Legion with Stan Laurel in hopes that I'll one day forget.

Figure 22-2
The same spreadsheet as in Figure 22-1, but opened as an e-mail attachment in Mail

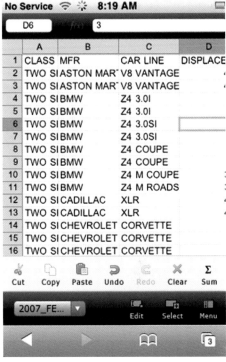

Figure 22-3
Real, honest-to-God, live spreadsheets on your iPhone, with EditGrid

that maybe I've had some form of stroke. Don't worry, it must have been a very mild one because all it did was knock out that section of my brain that's capable of seeing a link or a Web page announcing that Google Documents (http://docs.google.com) now supports the iPhone.

Yup, you're immediately making plans to start a telethon to raise funds for this disease. Because Google worked closely with Apple to ensure that a Google Maps widget is pre-installed on every iPhone. And (true story) a key member of the Google Reader development team waited in line all night to buy an iPhone the minute it went on sale, just

so he could race home and add changes to Google's newsfeed-reading service so it'd be more iPhone-studly.

Google Documents is one of the neatest services that Google provides. It's a complete suite of Microsoft Office-compatible apps that work through any browser. So of course http://docs.google.com is a useful link on *anyone's* browser, but on the most powerful smartphone in the world? Running the most powerful handheld Web browser anywhere? And the fact that Apple isn't officially allowing any third-party software to be developed? To say nothing of the fact that the iPhone's built-in spreadsheet reader doesn't allow you to edit spreadsheets and perform calculations, as the online Google Spreadsheet app does?

No, it *has* to be a stroke.

Just in case I haven't had a stroke, that this is in fact reality, and that Google actually *hasn't* supported the iPhone, I should point out that Google Documents is still a useful thing to know about. First and foremost, for you iPod Touch owners. You can't simply e-mail yourself a spreadsheet to view in the Mail app because you don't *have* a Mail app, do you?

But Google Documents has a few advantages for everybody. True, it doesn't reformat the spreadsheet to make it look nice on the iPhone screen, and you can't edit the data (that stinks, because natcherly, a spreadsheet is supposed to be a "live" document that can do math and stuff).

It still works well as a spreadsheet viewer. Figure 22-1 shows what a big spreadsheet looks like in Google Docs. Figure 22-2 shows what it looks like when it's opened as a Mail attachment. The Google version is already more readable — and I haven't even zoomed in yet.

Speed is the biggest improvement. This sample spreadsheet is a 500K monster, so you can forgive Mail for making me wait a minute or two before it's displayed. But scrolling around is like trying to pull a dead horse out of a bog.

There's also the convenience factor, of course. There are limits to how far you can go e-mailing spreadsheets to yourself. But if you keep data in Google Docs, you can upload new files to your account and access (and edit!) the spreadsheet data from any desktop in the world. And those files will be safe and sound until two days before Armageddon.

(Which, be fair, isn't a 48-hour span that you should be spending on office work. If there was ever a day to knock off work and take the kid to a ballgame, it's the day before the entire world is consumed in a lake of fire.)

In defense of the iPhone's built-in spreadsheet reader, I ought to remind you that it is indeed a system-wide resource and there are ways to store your spreadsheets that are *much* much more convenient than simply e-mailing files to yourself all the time. Check out Chapter 19 for the full story on ways to make your desktop files and data available on your iPhone.

EDITGRID TO THE RESCUE

No, if you truly want to open, read, *and* create *and* edit spreadsheets on your iPhone, you're gonna want to head to www.editgrid.com and sign up for an account.

EditGrid is the real deal on the iPhone or iPod Touch. When you point Safari at http://iphone.editgrid.com, you'll see an online spreadsheet app that is, frankly, incredible (see Figure 22-3). This is possibly one of the prettiest Safari based apps for the iPhone or iPod Touch, full-stop; the fact that it's doing something as sophisticated as running a real spreadsheet through a Web browser ups the awesome into the giga-Elvis spectrum.

Just dig all that attention to detail. And it's hands-down the fastest solution of all those available. It draws, scrolls, and redraws in a flash, and the developers paid such close attention to detail that you can even optimize the app's performance based on the complexity of the spreadsheet.

And (again) it's a *real* spreadsheet app. You can upload your desktop spreadsheets to the service (via your desktop browser), where they'll be available to your iPhone or iPod

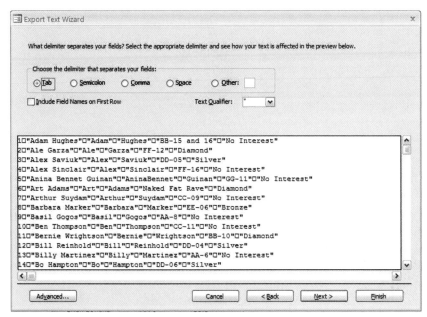

Figure 22-4

Turning database info into table data, which can then become a spreadsheet

Touch. You can create new documents. You can edit data, build new formula, and perform calculations and recalculations. It even charts!

Bookmark this, bookmark this, *bookmark this!*

ONWARD TO DATABASES

I'll begrudgingly cut the iPhone development team some slack for not including a database reader. Like I said earlier, there are just so many conflicting formats. And databases are more like live, complicated programs than simple, static mounds of data.

The best solution for taking your database data with you, then, is to transmogrify it so that it becomes a spreadsheet. Every database app allows you to export data into generic text-file formats in which every record in the database is a separate line and each record is separated by a tab (called "tab-delimited") or by a comma (which is why that specific flavor is called "CSV" — for "comma-separated values").

You then import this data into your spreadsheet app and save it as an Excel sheet. Many databases can even export your data directly into an Excel file, so you don't need to do any conversion at all. After you have a spreadsheet file, you can open and read it using whatever technique strikes your fancy, be it the iPhone's or iPod Touch's built-in reader or a great online app like EditGrid.

Figure 22-4 shows you what Microsoft Access's CSV export wizard looks like. You select the fields that you'd like the exported file to contain and it spits out a text file.

All those iPhone and iPod Touch ads. And

yet how does Apple choose to illustrate how
cool and exciting these devices are? By focus-
ing on (of all things!) the video player and
the iPod features and Safari.

Oh, please. As if a colorful, manic dance
video from the Koffs could ever be as exciting as an 865-row spreadsheet of crash
test data of midsize sedans equipped with
side-curtain airbags! Honestly, it's a world
gone mad. Well, even if Apple's unwilling
to promote the iPhone's ability to handle
this data, we members of the underground
alterna-actuarial groove scene can pitch in
with a grassroots effort. Keep independent
accounting alive!

23

Presentations

The Skim

PowerPoint Presentations ▪
Keynote Presentations

"We're opening a virtually untapped market, thanks to leveraging our vertical distribution paradigm across the manufacturing and actualization domains. With just $4.2 million in startup capitalization, fanning to $12.8 million over nine quarters with GMM linked to a platformed derivative, we're confident that your $900,000 VC investment in MartekLan will be one of the biggest success stories of the year.

"But don't take my word for it; we have all the breakdowns for you in a series of slides. Now, if you'll all just scoot in real close, I'll be using my phone's screen for the presentation. I hope none of you have a perfume sensitivity because I kind of went nuts with the Drakkar Noir this morning."

Yeah. Not likely. But with the addition of a $40 set of iPhone/iPod Touch video cables, loading your device with your presentation is a grand idea. It means that if you're making a quick trip to a conference room to just give this one presentation, you can travel across the building or across the world armed just with your pocket device and three or four feet or wire.

And as someone who spends a certain amount of time every year staring at 500 strange faces and being the only one in the room who (for these first few moments, anyway) realizes just how dumb the speaker actually is, putting you presentation on your iPhone or iPod Touch so you can run through it over and over again on the plane is often the difference between the conference organizers driving you to the airport afterwards in the back of a limo covered with glory and dumping you outside a bus station without your wallet or most of your clothing.

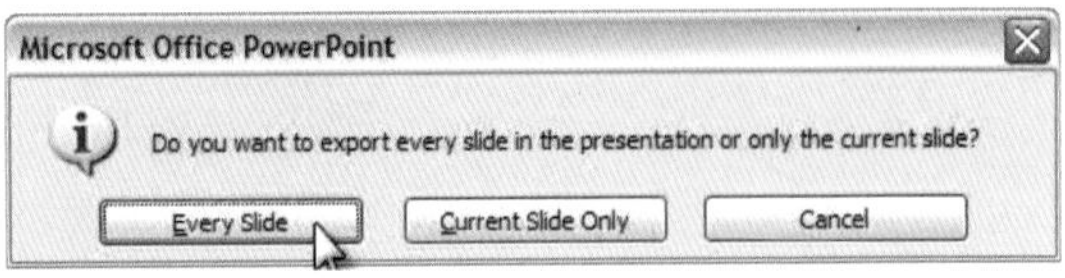

Figure 23-1
Telling PowerPoint to transmogrify the whole stack of slides

POWERPOINT PRESENTATIONS

Converting a PowerPoint presentation into a stack of images that we can savor in the iPhone's photo viewer app is a piece of cake. PowerPoint has a built-in ability to export a presentation as a series of JPEG files, so you're done and dusted with no added expenditures necessary.

To convert a PowerPoint presentation to a series of JPEG files:

1. Choose File ◆ Save As.
2. Choose JPEG File Interchange Format from the Save as Type pop-up menu in Windows or choose JPEG from the Format pop-up menu on the Mac.
3. Navigate to your My Pictures folder in Windows or Pictures on the Mac as the destination for the JPEGs, just to keep things tidy, and then click the Save button.
   - ◘ Note that the Windows edition will ask you if you want to export the entire presentation, or just the one slide you're looking at right now (see Figure 23-1). Click the Every Slide button.
   - ◘ Note that the Mac edition saves all the slides automatically; there is no option to choose just one slide.

And that's it. PowerPoint will grind its way through every one of your slides. The end result will be a brand-new folder with the exact same title as your presentation file, which will contain a sequence of JPEG files named something like Slide1, Slide2, Slide3, etc. (see Figure 23-2).

Now all you have to do is tell iTunes to synch your presentation folder to your iPhone the next time you update the device (see Figure 23-3). (Go to Chapter 20 for the complete 411 on loading images on your iPhone.)

And you're done. The presentation will appear under your iPhone's Photo Albums menu, listed by the name of the folder. So if the title of your presentation is "Jeff Gorman Is a Big Stupid Cheating Idiot Loser and Here's Why I Should Be the Commissioner of Our Fantasy Football League Instead" you *might* want to shorten the title of that folder to something that'll fit in the width of your iPhone's screen.

KEYNOTE PRESENTATIONS

Mac users have some extra mojo on their side: Apple makes the iPhone and Apple makes the OS and Apple makes its own presentation software (Keynote, part of the $79 iWorks suite), so all of those things tend to work together rather well.

In fact, if you peruse Keynote's export command (choose File ◆ Export), you'll find that the app can export your presentation

Figure 23-2
A big happy pile of JPEG slides

directly into iTunes in the form of a video file that you can synch to your iPhone or iPod Touch (see Figure 23-4).

And it's truly a one-click process. Click Next, specify a name for the new video file and a place to save it, and Keynote will bound off like a little bunny, rendering the

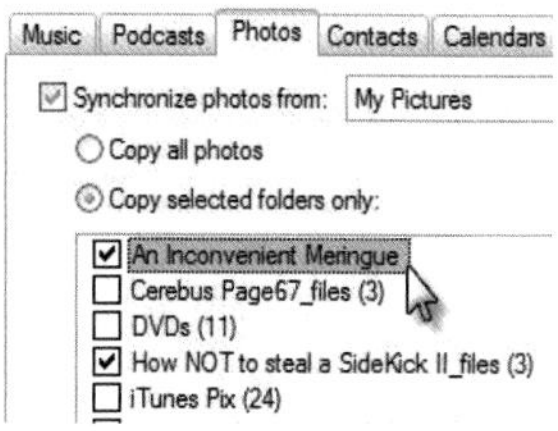

Figure 23-3
Plopping a presentation on your iPhone

presentation as a series of static images. When it's done, iTunes will activate, showing you the presentation video in the iTunes library. You can synch it to your iPhone or iPod Touch just like any other video file.

The advantage of this format is that it is indeed a video. So if you set up any sort of tricky visual transitions and effects (to distract people's attention from the horrifying news about the company's last quarter), they'll all show up in the video file.

The *downside* is that the iPhone and iPod Touch don't really recognize that a presentation is something that tends to stop and start

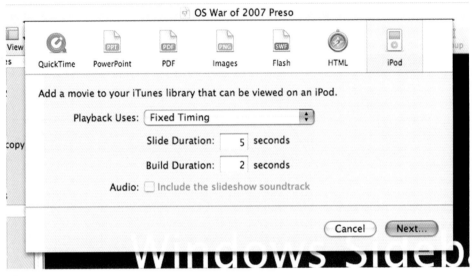

Figure 23-4
Apple Keynote hands off to Apple iTunes and thence to Apple iPhone.

after each slide. So when it's finished building your magic pie chart, it'll pause a few seconds (defined by the Duration setting in Keynote, as shown in Figure 23-4) and then move on, with or without you. So you'll have to manually tap the Pause button after each slide to hold it there, and then tap again to proceed.

For this reason, you might want to experiment with the simpler Export to Images feature, shown in Figure 23-5.

It's the same deal as when exporting JPEG files from PowerPoint. It spits out a stack of numbered JPEGs, which you can then synch to your iPhone or iPod Touch via its Photo Albums feature. (Again, check out Chapter 20 for the complete dope on using pictures.)

The slideshow feature of the iPhone or iPod Touch makes it simple to control the pace of the slides. Plus, because it *is* a stack of images, it's easy to go back to the album view, look at the entire presentation as a

series of thumbnails, and just tap on any one slide of interest, or start the presentation from any place you want.

As a man who never boards a plane with anything less than the same metric tonnage of equipment and technology that Arnold Schwarzenegger carries with him when he sets off to single-handedly destroy an entire drug cartel, the idea of traveling with nothing more than the entertainment player and e-mail/Web device that I carry around all the time anyway is awesomely seductive.

But consider the effect upon your audience.

Oh, right: I should point out that the video that your iPhone spits out will be "TV" resolution at best. Which is about a third to a quarter as sharp as what people would be seeing if you'd lugged your five-pound notebook all the way there.

What I actually was getting at was the possible resentment people might feel as you delicately unplug your iPhone and stick it back in

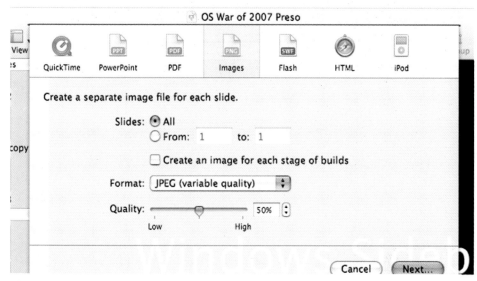

Figure 23-5
A less-sophisticated but simpler-to-use result: exporting to individual pictures

your hip pocket after the presentation.

"He's closing down a regional office that's been here for fifty years," your audience might be thinking. "I might lose my house, my kids might not be able to go to college, and *this* guy didn't want to inconvenience himself by taking an actual *notebook* with him on the plane?"

I wasn't there when the red banner of revolution threw the tsar out of power (my alibi is airtight, no matter what scandalous garbage you might have read on Wikipedia). But I imagine it was stuff exactly like this that finally pushed the huddled masses past the breaking point.

Index